Detroit Style
PIZZA
• A Doughtown History •

KAREN DYBIS

AMERICAN PALATE

Published by American Palate
A Division of The History Press
Charleston, SC
www.historypress.com

First published 2023

Manufactured in the United States

ISBN 9781467151948

Library of Congress Control Number: 2022951507

Notice: The information in this book is true and complete to the best of our knowledge. It is offered without guarantee on the part of the author or The History Press. The author and The History Press disclaim all liability in connection with the use of this book.

Much of pizza history is topped with a great deal of folklore, speculation and family tradition.

—John Arena, co-founder of Metro Pizza, Guinness World Record holder and World Pizza Champions team member

To Detroit—its people, its history, its pizza

CONTENTS

CONTENTS

INTRODUCTION

*M*ix your grandmother's kitchen with a basement rec room, and you have the essence of Buddy's Pizza at Six Mile and Conant in Detroit. It is the birthplace of Detroit Style pizza and a landmark to generations of Metro Detroiters.

If you've never been, Buddy's is a classic corner restaurant. You walk in under an awning and into a hallway made of wood paneling and cinder block. That's where you'll find the mural of the Supreme Court, the nickname for the women who ran Buddy's like their own, including Anna, Connie, Louisa, Dee, Sabina and Mary.

Climb the first set of stairs, and you enter a dining room with tables covered in checkerboard tablecloths. You will see young families drinking Faygo or retirees sharing a salad with Connie's famous dressing. Classic Motown music plays in the background, maybe Smokey Robinson crooning about cruising or the Temptations praising "My Girl." You're right by the kitchen, and its clatter fills the room.

Take the next set of stairs down into the bar, where the wood paneling picks up again along the booth-lined walls. By now, the scent of yeasty dough is hitting your nose, and your stomach starts to growl. Keep going into the next space, known as the Card Room. This is where decades of couples played pinochle while their kids made up games to pass the time. Around that corner is the patio room with murals for Vernors and other local favorites. Outside, you can see the bocce ball courts where people played throughout the day, sipping on coffee or boombas full of beer.

Metro Detroiters have played hundreds of rounds of pinochle and other card games inside of Buddy's Pizza, giving one of its side areas the nickname "the Card Room" for good reason. *Buddy's Pizza.*

These spaces are why Buddy's is one of Detroit's most beloved restaurants. The waitstaff were legendary, including women like Lu, Tex, Ila, Barb, Fran, Gloria, Charlene and Dottie. In those early days, bartenders like Robert Jacobs or Wes Pikula prepared shots of the waitstaff's favorite spirits, ready for them when they stopped by for an order. Managers including the venerable Irv Sosnick kept everyone moving, knowing every customer was there for something special. The kitchen was filled with high-spirited chefs and dough men like Gus, Louis and Dominick, jostling for space and moving fast to get orders out.

People have walked these floors for nearly a century now, starting with a small house that turned into a luncheonette and then into a beer garden and then, finally, a pizzeria that would become mythological both to the Motor City and, later, to the culinary world.

It's Buddy's, and it feels like home.

Like many people born and raised in Michigan, I knew square pizza was something unique to Metro Detroit. Everyone ate this red-topped pie on special occasions; it was something you asked for on your birthday. I appreciated how it was different than the everyday round pizza. Square pizza had a fluffy doughiness with a tomato sauce that was a perfect balance of acid and sweetness.

The star was, of course, the corner slice. It was the stuff of culinary dreams: that deep, soul-satisfying, grilled-toast crunch and caramelized flavor. As my world expanded and new pizzerias opened, my taste for square pizza remained true.

In recent years, this Metro Detroit mainstay went from a local favorite to a national and then international sensation. Seemingly overnight, the square pie locals knew and loved became known as "Detroit Style pizza," with pizzerias from Austin to Denver to San Francisco and New York making their versions. Soon enough, Detroit-style pizza had spread to Toronto, Mexico, England, the Philippines and Dubai, making it a worldwide treat.

At the same time, online recipes for Detroit Style populated across cooking websites. Instagram posts showing images of the perfect square with impossibly high cheese crowns proliferated. Chat rooms, Facebook pages and YouTube channels filled with tributes to the crunch, the taste and the people who were obsessed with making it.

That led to the question: What changed in the years since Buddy's started serving its square pizza in 1946 that made Detroit Style so popular? Was this adoration for the square pie just a trend, or had Detroit Style become part of the pizza history books? Had Detroit Style earned its spot next to other styles such as New York, New Haven, Chicago and others? And who were the people responsible for this amazing transformation, taking the square pie from a Detroit thing and launching it into the mainstream, into cookbooks, onto television shows, across social media and into appreciative stomachs around the world?

Buddy's waitstaff, with their unique personalities, became part of the entertainment of going to the restaurant at Six Mile and Conant. Some of the most recognizable members of its staff included women like Lu, Tex, Ila, Barb, Fran, Gloria, Charlene and Dottie. *Buddy's Pizza.*

That drive to discover just what Detroit Style is introduced me to local pizza royalty, or what *Detroit News* food writer Melody Baetens calls "the holy trinity of historic Detroit Style pizza parlors." These are the cooks and families who have worked elbow deep in flour, San Marzano tomatoes, Wisconsin brick cheese and freshly sliced pepperoni for decades.

These original pizza makers worked hard to survive, fought to keep the recipe intact (and largely a secret) and sought to keep the traditions going in a way that deserves admiration and respect. They're still fighting that fight—a struggle that speaks to the challenges Detroit itself has faced because people outside of the Midwest decided they know more about a city and its pizza than those who created it.

This journey took me to the innovators: the chefs and Metro Detroiters who introduced square pizza to other palates and other people. In some cases, they went to culinary school or worked for one of the originals, while others are self-taught. Some moved out of Michigan for one reason or another, mostly for economic opportunities that took them to places like Texas and Colorado. They met in places like San Francisco for pizza classes

Buddy's Rendezvous started as a home and developed over time into a luncheonette, beer garden and, with the addition of pizza, a pizzeria, thanks to Gus Guerra and his mother-in-law's recipe. *Author's collection.*

and, later, Las Vegas for pizza competitions. These were the people who put in the hours to educate their customers about Detroit, its pizza history, its culinary innovations and the greatness of that corner slice.

My trek toward pizza knowledge also led me to find the experts and the next generation of Detroit Style pizza devotees: the chefs who know modern techniques that have elevated this humble pie in important ways. This led to the companies who adapted Detroit Style to serve their menus and goals as well as the investors who saw an opportunity to grow this trend into a lucrative business. I came to realize that Detroit Style was now a permanent part of the pizza universe, and that was something new—and it was still developing in a way that deserved documenting.

All along this route, I became increasingly fascinated with pizza, the pizzaiolos who devote their lives to perfecting this food and the industry that supports creativity and innovation. To research this book, I've eaten pizza across my home state and across the world, traveling far and wide, even to its homeland of Italy. It's hard work, but someone has to eat all those delicious pies. What I learned along the way is you can't help but cheer for these devoted makers, and you feel their pain when life happens or infighting causes rifts that may never be healed. Pizza is one of those rare foods that when you decide to learn more about it, you get drawn deeper into the people and the practice. Making a perfect pizza may be the end goal, but the process of getting there is educational, frustrating, entertaining and, ultimately, deeply satisfying.

The goal of this book is twofold. First, you will want to eat every pizza and visit every pizzeria mentioned. Second, now that you also know the history and feel connected to why and how this pizza style was created, you will seek to preserve the past while appreciating the innovations that undoubtedly will continue.

Detroit Style pizza started in the Motor City. Detroit deserves the credit and, most importantly, the respect for creating such a perfect pie. It's more than its shape or its pizza lineage. It goes beyond a simple Sicilian square. It evolved out of this region's expertise in food, storytelling and entrepreneurialism. And it will continue to feed people for decades and, hopefully, beyond—because it is just that good.

Chapter 1

WHAT IS DETROIT STYLE PIZZA?

*T*he history of a food is as rich and complex as the people who make it. If it is made with the best ingredients available, seasoned well, presented beautifully and tastes like nothing else you've ever had before, it becomes memorable, celebrated and venerated. It also gets imitated, experimented with and updated.

So, what is Detroit Style pizza? The answer is both simple and complex.

The simple part is how the style originated. In the beginning, a San Marino immigrant named Gus Guerra made a singular pizza meant to stand out from his competitors for a restaurant he co-owned called Buddy's Rendezvous in Detroit. His family says the recipe came from his mother-in-law, and he and his wife, Anna, perfected it over many years of practice. At its core, Detroit Style is a little bit Sicilian and a little bit San Marino. It is likely based on the *sfincione*, a traditional Sicilian street pizza topped with onions, anchovy paste, breadcrumbs and tomato sauce, creating a salty, umami taste bomb. Guerra's pizza is said to have had a light yet chewy crust, cheese all the way to the edges of a rectangular, high-walled pan and tomato sauce on top.

On the complex side, Detroit Style has developed since Guerra created it in 1946 into a series of qualities that are hotly discussed, dissected and debated. This includes the dough and how it is made, the layering of ingredients and the type of cheese and the way it is applied, as well as the method and timing of how the pizza maker applies the sauce.

Here are the general attributes of a Detroit Style pizza:

Detroit Style pizza is defined in part by its square or rectangular shape, its high-walled pan with slightly angled sides and the sauce on top. *Buddy's Pizza.*

The first layer: It starts with a simple dough of salt, water, yeast and flour. That's it. Some people add oil; others do not. Traditionally, it is a high-hydration dough, which means the water-to-flour ratio is greater than that of the average pizza dough.

The second layer: Pepperoni is pressed into the dough, which some say adds fat and flavor. Guerra first sliced his pepperoni by hand or on a wall-mounted slicer.

The third layer: Brick cheese, a style of cheese known and made mostly in Wisconsin, is applied over the dough and pepperoni. Some makers use a blend of brick cheese and mozzarella. Some use mozzarella and another cheese, like a cheddar. The cheese is typically chopped into small cubes or shredded. The cheese should be applied with a gentle touch so it does not compress the dough and it should be spread to the edges of the pan, so that when the dough bakes into the corners, it becomes crispy.

The fourth layer: A light tomato sauce is flicked off the end of a spoon or lightly ladled on top of the cheese. Those who prefer the ladle technique tend to apply it in long stripes. This can be done before or after the pizza is baked. Depending on the pizza maker, the sauce may be cold, room temperature or warmed. What is key is that the sauce should be equally distributed and touch every slice of pizza.

The pans: Detroit Style is traditionally made in a pan with high walls that lean out at a slight angle. Guerra says he used pans he brought from home; his family says he bought them later from a hardware store. Many pizzerias use pans purchased from a manufacturer who intended them to be oil-drip trays or automotive parts containers; some buy pans from pizza-pan manufacturers.

The result: The combination of Guerra's original recipe with these pans results in a light, chewy dough that is higher and thicker than that of a round pizza and has crispy, cheesy corners that are addictive. How many toppings you add or when in the process you add them is debatable, but many makers have shifted the toppings, including the pepperoni, to the top of the pizza but still under the sauce.

What about those pans? There are multiple theories about where Guerra got his pans. Did Guerra get his pans from an automotive factory or from a customer who worked in a plant? Or did he get them from family or buy them in a store? Just like the rest of Detroit Style pizza lore, this one is up for debate.

What is a pizzaiolo? It is a term the pizza industry uses to describe someone who is slavishly devoted to making the best pizza he or she possibly can. They may have a culinary degree, they may be trained to make a specific style or they may be self-taught.

The corner slice is considered the most important area of a Detroit Style pizza because its caramelized cheese forms a *frico*, or crunchy crust. *Buddy's Pizza.*

Where did the term "Detroit Style" come from? Although most people started using "Detroit Style" in the early to mid-2010s to describe the city's square pizza, it actually was first used in the 1980s in publications such as the *Detroit News*. Later, the term was used infrequently in pizza-industry magazines; most of these references were to Buddy's Pizza or Cloverleaf. The term gained real traction nationally between 2010, when Tony Gemignani added this style to his menu in San Francisco, and 2011, when two Metro Detroit brothers named Brandon and Zane Hunt opened a pizza trailer in Austin, Texas, introducing "Detroit Style pizza" as a descriptor in a real and substantive way. The term skyrocketed in usage over time after a pizzaiolo named Shawn Randazzo won a major Las Vegas pizza competition in 2012 and opened a business using that term in its name.

This book has chosen to capitalize the term "Detroit Style" to honor its historical significance. It also highlights the recognition within the pizza industry that Detroit ranks among cities including Chicago, New York, New Haven and others in having a significant pizza style.

Some say Metro Detroiters like Gus and Anna Guerra, the Hunt brothers and Shawn Randazzo changed the pizza world forever. But there were people who came before them, and there are people who came after them who have made major contributions to the pizza world. We know some of their names; others are lost to history. But they all had a hand in making Detroit Style what it is.

The result is a messy, chaotic and dramatic history. And what a delicious story it is.

Chapter 2

THE THREE WAVES

*D*etroit Style Pizza started with the Guerra family, and it became a worldwide sensation. How? The first break came when Guerra and his partners sold the business and Guerra shared his recipe with the new owners. Guerra then opened a new restaurant with his recipe. Later branches of this family tree came about when family or friends working at Buddy's or Cloverleaf left to re-create the recipe at another restaurant. Then, the advent of the Internet and social media spread its gospel as people moved out of Detroit and new people discovered it.

This went on and on for decades, forming three waves of Detroit Style pizza. Each wave tells the story of humble beginnings and has all the drama of a television soap opera—and it all comes from one pizza style.

The First Wave

The first wave began in 1946 and continued to about 1970. It began with August "Gus" Guerra when he brought his mother-in-law's recipe and bread pans to work for the first time. Guerra owned a restaurant with his wife's two uncles, and when they split, he created the first of many divisions in Detroit Style pizza. Guerra sold Buddy's to friends, waited for a bit and then opened his own restaurant in a bar known as Clover Leaf in East Detroit, where he served nearly the same recipe. The second sale of Buddy's Pizza in the 1970s to the Jacobs family resulted in another branch

Gus Guerra came to the United States from San Marino in hopes of having a better life here, working with family and developing multiple small businesses. *Guerra family.*

on the tree—that is when longtime pizzaiolo Louis Tourtois left to work at a nearby bar called Shield's and began making his version of the recipe. A 1970 *Detroit News* pizza contest established Buddy's as the area's top pie, setting up a rivalry between Buddy's, Shield's and the new Cloverleaf pizzeria. Later that decade, Tourtois left Shield's to open Loui's Pizza, creating additional rivalries. Competition was so intense that these chefs refused to share their recipes with anyone. Meanwhile, newcomers sought out information through high and low methods, including dumpster diving, to figure out what ingredients these original makers used.

During these years, Detroit gained fame and attention for its pizza prowess, largely due to round-pizza makers. This list includes pizza dynasties including Domino's, Little Caesars and other significant chain or commodity pie makers such as Dino's and more. Local brands who served a blend of round and square gained fans, including Green Lantern, Nikki's and Buscemi's. They knew the public's tastes, temperaments and economic pain points. More importantly, they knew how to use this knowledge for profit, growing pizza companies that rank among the top in the nation in terms of revenue and employment. Building this perfect round pie took years of perseverance and dedication. But when these creators got it right, they became millionaires and gave Detroit another pizza crown to wear, albeit a slightly different one than Detroit Style.

THE SECOND WAVE

The second wave lasted from about 1970 to 2016. This is when a confluence of larger-than-life personalities with a connection to Metro Detroit started to talk among themselves about square pizza. They debated how they could learn to make it and how they could develop businesses to sell it. These ambitious and competitive people knew there was something special about the deep-dish pizza they loved from Buddy's, Cloverleaf, Shield's and an up-and-coming carryout pizzeria chain called Jet's that they wanted to re-create. What bonded them was that they wanted the rest of the world to understand and appreciate Detroit's square pie, something that separated them from the first-wave originators.

The conversations Brandon and Zane Hunt were having with pizza makers brought them in contact with Shawn Randazzo, who was working for Cloverleaf and the Guerra family. This friendship blossomed through emails, telephone calls and in-person conversations, creating a prototype

Shawn Randazzo worked for Cloverleaf for more than fifteen years before launching his own business, Detroit Style Pizza Company. He earned multiple pizza-making awards while at both jobs, including World Pizza Champion. *Randazzo family.*

for a pizza community. Their paths started to cross in real life when the Hunts took their idea for a pizza business out of their dreams and into reality by attending pizza expos in Las Vegas and a pizza-training class in San Francisco. There, the Hunt brothers met two key people: Influential pizza master Tony Gemignani and an emerging pizza maker from Metro Detroit, Jeff Smokevitch. These second-wave makers worked together to figure out the formula and technique, unlocking it for the greater world.

THE THIRD WAVE

The third wave started around 2016, reached a fever pitch in 2020 and continues into today. It largely started when a married couple looking to start their own pizza revolution decided to order a few frozen Buddy's pizzas to try at home. Thanks to their research, Emily and Matt Hyland knew they could use this pizza style as a platform to build something New York had never seen before. Their tribute to Detroit Style proved so successful that they were able to start a chain of restaurants with this pizza as its base.

Their success and a growing Internet drove chefs there and elsewhere to try Detroit Style—only to find the same inspiration. Add in the advent of social media, and an online explosion occurred. Soon, social media sites like Instagram and cookbooks like Gemignani's *Pizza Bible* gave people an idea of what those cheesy corners and signature saucy top could do for their menus. The fascination with Detroit Style continued to grow into 2020, when the coronavirus pandemic convinced amateur chefs who had perfected Detroit Style at home to open pop-up shops, pizza trailers and full-fledged restaurants serving the Detroit Style pizza they had grown to love. Chefs used pizza blogs, cookbooks and training programs from second-wave celebrities like Randazzo to make their own Detroit Style pies, which soon became internationally beloved.

Where does Detroit Style go from here? The future only knows.

Chapter 3

ABOUT THOSE PANS...

*F*or decades, people have told the Detroit Style pizza creation story as such: Gus Guerra and Buddy's Rendezvous used automotive parts pans to make square pizza.

The question is: How did he get those pans and why did he use them to make pizza? Did he get them from a customer who brought in some parts pans or drip pans from an auto plant?

Gus's family says one thing is true: they never asked Gus where the pans came from, so the ultimate answer is lost to history.

Here's what we do know: Gus did work for Ford Motor Company between 1940 and 1944 as a tile setter, so maybe he got a pan or two during that period. Maybe a friend brought a pan in for him to use once he started at Buddy's in 1944—although Gus didn't start making pizza until two years later.

Here's what is also true: as the business grew, Gus needed more and more pans. In those years, Gus bought his pans from hardware stores, including one owned by family friends, according to Jack and Marie Guerra Easterby, Gus Guerra's two surviving children.

Jack and Marie say they know their parents were close with John and Clotilde "Babe" Pini for decades; in fact, they called her Aunt Babe, and he was Uncle John. According to his newspaper obituary, John Pini owned Handy Hardware store on Nine Mile in Warren. Jack Guerra remembers going to this hardware store and others with his father, who swore him to secrecy as to what they were buying there—and it was those sacred pizza

Two of the things that make Detroit Style pizza pans unique are their high walls and angled sides, which help create the crunchy cheese crust on the outside of the pie. *Randazzo family*.

pans Guerra used to make Detroit Style. John Pini may have purchased the pans he sold to these pizzerias from Parkersburg Iron & Steel, which then became Dover Parkersburg.

It is likely that Buddy's Pizzeria, at one time, may also have purchased its pans from John Pini at his hardware store. Babe's brother was James Bonacorsi, who purchased Buddy's from Gus in 1953 and then ran it with his business partner James Valente until 1970.

According to Jack Guerra, "[My dad] told me what to do. He didn't tell me stories"—especially about the origins of the original pans. But Jack notes that there weren't many restaurant-supply stores available when his father started making pizzas at Buddy's in the late 1940s.

"Baking equipment that was available in the 1950s was very thin. They had the basics. There was not a lot of products out there for people to use," Jack Guerra says. So, in other words, you had to be creative with what was available at the time.

Without Gus here to answer, it may be true that he used automotive parts or drip pans to make his first Detroit Style pizza. It is a colorful bit of folklore that speaks to people, and it makes sense to those living in the Motor City. Lots of people "walk away" with items they find at work, and many of those items end up in people's homes or side businesses.

Many pizzerias that make Detroit Style today swear by these sorts of pans, but most are made for the pizza industry and never see the inside of an automotive plant or even an auto parts store.

Whether you use a bread pan, an automotive parts pan or whatever else you have around your house to make your Detroit Style pizza, all it needs to be is relatively square with high walls, and it likely will turn out just fine.

PART I

....

THE FIRST WAVE

Chapter 4

BUDDY'S RENDEZVOUS/
CLOVERLEAF PIZZA

*G*us Guerra was worn out, dogged by seemingly endless hours at Buddy's Rendezvous and a nagging feeling that something wasn't right. He had been in business with his wife's family for nearly a decade, but it still felt like they never made enough money.

Gus was working the bar, taking care of the regulars and making sure no one had too much to drink. His wife, Anna, was in the kitchen, making the pizza that had started giving them some margin so they could sleep at night. They both spent so much time at Buddy's that her mom practically lived at their house, taking care of their son, Frank, and, later, the twins, Jack and Marie.

Gus bought into the bar in 1944, becoming a business partner with Anna's uncles. Joe Genco owned the building with another family member, who wanted out. Joe needed a front man of sorts, and Gus was already naturalized, so he could help run the place. Joe's brother, Gaspar, was the third partner. Joe did the books, and in those days, everything was paid in cash on delivery. After all the bills and taxes were paid, they'd decide how much money was left over to split between the partners.

The truth about just how much money was going to one particular partner came out when Joe was in the hospital. Gus was incensed. He and Anna were working all hours, missing their kids' childhoods, only to find out they'd been cheated by family. Gus had known starvation, poverty and struggle from the moment he was born—and he didn't want that for his own children. He ended the partnership.

Gus found a pair of buyers eager to take over. The only thing left to do was figure out what he would do next. Gus still wanted to work, but Buddy's new owners wanted him out of the city entirely. The new owners didn't want to split up the customers, who might stay loyal to Gus if he were too close.

In the span of a few months, Gus went from a respected businessman to a guy with no steady job and a family to feed. He needed to find somewhere else to work—and soon. Finding something that fit as well as Buddy's would take a lot of searching, and Gus was still dealing with the fallout from the split.

How did he go from the top of his game to the bottom again?

AGOSTINO GUERRA WAS BORN October 9, 1908, in San Marino, a small republic in northern Italy. His father, Francesco, was a farmer, and his mother, Maria Gennari, was a homemaker. Like many young men of his era, Gus chose to take his chances in the United States and set sail on the

Agostino Guerra was born on October 9, 1908, in San Marino, a small republic in northern Italy. His father, Francesco, was a farmer, and his mother, Maria Gennari, was a homemaker. *Guerra family.*

Agustin from Genoa, Italy. He was alone, and he likely wondered what kind of life he was about to have in this new country.

His son, Jack, says anything was likely better than what Gus was leaving behind.

"In the old country, you'd get up, go to work and you'd work on a farm from dawn to dusk. You'd get paid one loaf of bread for the day and that's it. Nothing else," Jack says. "Dad was one of seven kids. He had a sister who died, and there were six brothers. They were very poor. There was nothing you could do about it."

Gus arrived in the United States on March 19, 1929, with less than one hundred dollars in his pocket. He started out in Sandusky, Ohio, staying with family while he worked in a nearby quarry. Gus rarely spoke about those early years other than to say he struggled. Longtime Cloverleaf general manager Carol Corrie says Gus told her he had such a meager existence then he didn't even own a coat. "Gus was the poorest of the poor," Carol says.

Gus moved to Detroit, where he worked a series of jobs, including as a tile setter for Ford Motor Company. On his World War II draft card, Gus said he was living on Le May Street with his cousin, Joe. According to the card's registrar's report, Gus was white with a light complexion, brown hair and brown eyes. He stood five feet, seven inches tall and weighed approximately 170 pounds.

GUS MET ANNA PASSALACQUA when they were matched by friends, the kind who know you well and have a good idea you'd work as a couple. "They got set up on a blind date by Nino and Lina Uberti, San Marino friends," says Gus's daughter, Marie Guerra Easterby. "That's how they met back then was through introductions."

Anna seemed like the right woman for Gus. She was from a good family who owned a grocery store on Heidelberg in Detroit, so she understood money, and she was independent-minded. Was it love at first sight? Only they know. Their *Detroit Free Press* engagement announcement listed Gus as thirty-two and Anna as twenty-seven—a couple old enough to be practical but still excited for their future.

Gus and Anna married on November 21, 1940. It was a time marked with tragedy—Anna's brother, Frank, had just passed away, and Anna was in mourning. The couple married at Holy Family Church and held a dinnertime reception at the Bowery in Detroit. Their honeymoon in

Gus Guerra and Anna Passalacqua married in November 1940. They were set up by their best friends, Nino and Lina Uberti, who also stood up in their wedding. *Guerra family.*

Sandusky included a few days visiting Gus's cousins, who taught Anna some of their San Marino recipes. Little is known of their first years of marriage, but that's likely the sign of a successful start. In November 1943, they had their first son, Frank August Guerra. By 1944, Gus was making about seventy dollars a week at Ford.

But family was calling him in another direction—they needed help at their beer garden. Anna's uncles, Joe and Gasper Genco, owned the little place at 17125 Conant Avenue with another partner, who wanted out of the deal. Gus was a naturalized citizen, and they needed him in order to get a liquor license. Jack and Marie say their father's initial investment was $2,300, and the potential profits had to be split three ways.

The challenge was how to make enough money. One idea was to add food. It had to be something easy to make, cheap to put together and able to feed a crowd. It's likely the family talked it over at multiple meals together, debating ideas. Anna's mother, the Sicilian matriarch Crucificia "Celia" Passalacqua, had a lifetime of cooking to serve as experience. But

Celia also had an understanding of the grocery business, something that likely made her wise enough to suggest a food that was economical as well as easy to prepare.

It was pizza. Specifically, her pizza. And it came in one shape: square.

PIZZA WAS HARDLY A new dish when Gus started making it. Many cultures have flatbread with a sauce or toppings on it as a relatively inexpensive food offering. Conventional wisdom dates the dish as we know it to Naples, Italy, likely sometime around the early 1700s. Pizza, back then, was a simple street food—it was highly portable, as you could take a slice with you as you walked to work or home for the night.

Italian immigration brought pizza to the United States, likely around the late 1800s. According to pizza historian Peter Regas, the modern-day pizzeria started as an Italian bakery. These bakeries already had the ingredients and the equipment needed to make pizza as a way to feed themselves or make a little extra money. "It was a bread business with a side of pizza," Regas says.

New York earns the distinction of having the first U.S. pizzerias, Regas says. The density of Italians in New York as well as other cities such as Chicago and Detroit brought pizza into these growing metropolises. Pizza got even more interesting as taverns started serving it as a side dish to the drinks they slung, especially post-Prohibition, Regas says. Tavern owners didn't have the constraints of a bakery background, so they could make whatever they wanted and change the recipe as it suited them. Plus, they wanted something that was cheap to make and tasted good. Pizza continued to evolve as people of all backgrounds got married and started making pizza together, blending cultures and food traditions.

"There were hundreds of pizzerias in the United States before World War II, so it's not soldiers coming back that boost[ed] the industry," Regas says. "But they did come home and demand pizza."

Detroit is a classic case of Italian bakeries offering up pizza as a cost-effective dish to serve larger groups. Its first mention in a major Detroit newspaper came in March 1939, describing the "poor man's pie" as a Philadelphia favorite. "Beer is a friendly follower of this Neapolitan pie that is pronounced 'peetza.' Its popularity has sauced the opening of some 17 pizzarias [sic] or pizza bakeries in the last 18 months," the story notes. Months later, in August 1939, *Detroit Free Press* reporter Gertrude Voellmig mentioned visiting an Italian bakery and trying pizza. Voellmig, a Wayne State University graduate who became a food writer and cookbook author, describes the unnamed bakery as "neater than a pin just removed from a fresh box" and a bread shop of note.

Voellmig calls pizza a "fascinating thing," made with sweet Italian dough. It is "spread out into a long thin layer. Over the top is spread a delicious mixture of cheese (mainly goat I was told), imported olive oil, fish and a number of other ingredients we couldn't mention without giving away the recipe secret. Last of all the whole thing is dotted with thin slices of a peppy Italian sausage and baked in the oven." The resulting food is a novelty she recommends to women throwing parties. "A huge one—enough for at least 25 guests—sells for $1. You can get them in halves for 50 cents," Voellmig says.

By 1943, one of Detroit's first pizzerias was getting rave reviews from *Detroit Free Press* cosmopolitan editor Paul Deao. The reporter visited Pizzeria Vesuvio, a popular restaurant at 3001 Gratiot owned by Philip Migliore. According to the article, Migliore

Crucificia "Celia" Passalacqua (*right*) is said to have provided the basic recipe that became Detroit Style pizza, basing it on her knowledge of Sicilian pizza making. *Guerra family.*

was an auto worker who saw a letter on the *Freep*'s food page complaining there was no place in the city to get a good slice of pizza. Migliore invested in his restaurant, and the rest, as they say, is history. When asked what pizza is, Migliore explains: "You take plain bread dough and spread it out 12 inches in diameter and one quarter of an inch thick. Then cover it with sliced tomatoes, a layer of sliced, dry sausage, mozzarella cheese or anchovies; add mushrooms; give it a good sprinkle of Roman type cheese and olive oil and bake it for 10 minutes. That should give you a treat a la Napolitana."

GUS KNEW VESUVIO'S PIZZA. To stand out against potential competitors, Gus probably decided making a pizza more like his mother-in-law's gave him a better chance of getting noticed. Other bars in the area were focusing on dishes like fish and chips in an effort to draw in soldiers returning from World War II. Where Migliore was making a round, thin crust, Gus and Anna focused on a thick, square Sicilian pizza, similar to a *sfincione*.

Left: The base for Detroit Style pizza is the *sfincione*. This pizza is traditionally made on a rimmed sheet pan, which gives the dough room to rise and creates a thicker crust. *Author's collection.*

Below: *Sfinguini*, like this one at Bommerito's Bakery in St. Clair Shores, features a thick crust, tomato sauce, onions, Parmesan cheese and olive oil. *Author's collection.*

Referred to as the original Sicilian pizza, *sfincione* is traditionally made on a rimmed sheet pan, which gives the dough room to rise and creates a thicker crust. The usual toppings are a blend of tomato sauce, cheese, diced onions and anchovies. If you need to, you can stretch that topping out even more by adding some olive oil or a cup of bread crumbs. Gus's mother-in-law likely made *sfincione* at home as a cost-conscious supper. But it was also made in Sicilian bakeries of her era as something to sell to a hungry working man who wanted a taste of home and a quick meal.

Gus likely saw the *sfincione* as an answer to a prayer. The bar needed a food he or Anna could make themselves. It needed to be inexpensive with readily available ingredients, things he could pick up from any small grocer. Ideally, serving the bar patrons something salty meant they'd drink more, something that could help the overall business.

Innately, Gus probably knew Buddy's patrons would not be familiar with *sfincione* or come from a Sicilian background. They might balk at eating a pizza they weren't familiar with or might not want that anchovy taste, for example. He and Anna probably started experimenting with the recipe, cutting out whatever they could to save a penny or two. The result would be more palatable to American tastes and keep the old-world recipe cost effective. But to keep it looking the same, Gus may have kept the sauce on top as a nod to his mother-in-law or as a way to keep the peace in the family if she found out he had changed her recipe. Plus, keeping the sauce on top maintained a light, crunchy crust, giving the pizza a shape and flavor unlike his nearby competitors'.

Best of all, Gus told *A Taste of Pizza* magazine, he could use equipment readily available to him, so his startup costs were minimal.

"We used to make bread in those pans at home," Gus said. "My wife's mother used to make it at home, and she used the same formula we use now; basically, a bread recipe."

For a likely desperate Gus and his fledgling enterprise, this new kind of *sfincione*-meets-American pizza looked and tasted like a winner.

THE AREA AROUND BUDDY'S was Polish and Italian, mostly men who worked in the automotive industry as blue-collar workers of one type or another, Gus told *A Taste of Pizza* in one of his most extensive interviews about his early years at Buddy's and then Cloverleaf. "There is a high concentration of people in this area from San Marino, particularly in East Detroit, Roseville and Harper Woods. I think this has something to do with the way pizza grew here."

To get new customers, Buddy's advertised in the newspapers, but most of the customers found it through word of mouth, Gus said. "Oftentimes, we would make up a couple of pizzas and pass them around the bar for snacks. This really helped."

In those days, Gus told *A Taste of Pizza* that supplies weren't too dear. Mozzarella was around fifty cents a pound; pepperoni was about sixty-six cents a pound. "We used Kraft cheese, Casino brand. Things were pretty inexpensive then, and our pizzas sold cheap," Gus said. "We weren't making a lot of money, just enough to make ends meet. And take care of family needs. It was quite a struggle years ago, before pizza was recognized."

In a 1981 interview with the *Detroit News*, Gus said the pizza was built just like Grandma Passalacqua taught: thick crust, pepperoni, mushrooms, Casino brick cheese, the extras and "finally a dabbing of tomato sauce. 'And my pizza hasn't changed much to this day,' says Gus."

Gus also told *A Taste of Pizza* that Anna was his saving grace at Buddy's and Cloverleaf. "I needed my wife's help, but at first the babies were too small, only about two years old. They weren't even four when she started to work in the kitchen, making the pizzas by hand. I would help a little. We didn't have a dough mixer then," Gus said. "Usually, I worked behind the bar and she took phone calls, made and baked the pizzas, and delivered them to the tables....Grandma took care of the children when we got busy."

Jack Guerra backs this up: "My dad would start work at seven in the morning and leave at two thirty or three thirty in the morning after the place was clean and then go back to work again and open up at seven in the morning. He was never home. He always worked."

Marie agrees: "My mom always worked, too. I remember her always in a white uniform....If grandma couldn't watch us, we'd sit in the back room and fall asleep."

Some stories about Buddy's Rendezvous mention another woman working in the kitchen back in 1946, specifically Buddy's employee Connie Piccinato. The myth of Connie working with Gus in 1946 started when Connie told a *Crain's Detroit* freelance reporter in the 1980s that she was there at the beginning. However, Jack and Marie Guerra refute this, saying that is impossible based on what they know of their parents and the way the business was run. Besides their testimony, there is ample documentation that indicates Connie was not in the kitchen alongside Gus Guerra, including her son's account of her life, her newspaper obituary (which says she started at Buddy's in 1952) and U.S. Census data that shows she was not working at Buddy's in or before 1950.

Gus and Anna Guerra worked long days and nights at Buddy's Rendezvous and, later, at Cloverleaf, the pizzeria they opened in East Detroit; the city later became known as Eastpointe. *Guerra family.*

"My mother never would have let her in there," Jack says. "My father was always honest with me. He never lied to me in my life. I know if there had been someone else there, he would have told me. I never heard [Connie's] name before. Never."

"Dad felt he wasn't making enough money with two silent partners. And to have her come in where there's Grandma, Mama and maybe Aunt Virginia? Why would they hire a strange woman?" Marie Guerra Easterby says.

THE DETAILS AROUND THE end of the Buddy's partnership between Gus Guerra, Gaspar Genco and Joe Genco are a bit muddy due to time. But according to Jack Guerra and Marie Easterby Guerra, Gus agreed in 1953 during the separation not to open a competing pizzeria within two miles of Buddy's. After all, people tend to use location as the key reason they pick a place to eat, and Jimmy Bonacorsi and Jimmy Valente were smart enough to know that if the original pizza maker was anywhere nearby, they might not get the business they needed to survive. Gus understood. After all, he had taught Big Jimmy and Little Jimmy how to make the recipe, and if Gus was like most chefs of his era, he told them some but not all of his secrets. Gus also included his cook, Dominick, in the deal; Dominick would go on to train one of Buddy's most famous chefs, Louis Tourtois.

"Buddy's is competition today. But since people are very mileage-minded now, if they're closer to us, they'll probably come here. If they're closer to Buddy's, they'll probably go there," Gus told *A Taste of Pizza.*

By late April, Gus had found a little bar in East Detroit for sale. The Clover Leaf was an Irish pub, and it looked like a white farmhouse sitting out in the middle of a field. The building was rough, with a small vestibule entrance that led into the main bar and seating area. Gus described the interior as needing some work, noting that "the floors were rocky" and "the building itself was 75 or 80 years old."

Gus got a $30,000 loan from his friend, businessman Henry "Hank" Vettraino, to buy Cloverleaf. Gus told Vettraino he would pay him back, and he was good on that promise. It took from April to December of that year to get the new Cloverleaf opened as a pizzeria, Jack says.

"My mom worked in the back; she did the pizzas. My dad tended bar," Jack says. "Everyone who was here was friendly. By 3:00 p.m., they'd be lined up and [start] walking in the door. There was one guy, an old German man named Pete, who worked for a tool and die. He'd come in every day, five days a week, Monday through Friday. He'd have three shots of chilled Kessler whiskey, talk for a while and then go home to his wife for dinner. That's what people did back then. They were all done for the day, and now it was time to relax."

Cloverleaf grew as people started coming in, looking for nearby pizza but also for Gus and Anna. They also wanted the original pizza, but even Gus knew that subtle changes happened from time to time. When asked if the pizzas he made at Cloverleaf were the same as the ones at Buddy's, Gus was pragmatic about it: "It's somehow different. It's pretty hard to keep a recipe without adding your own changes to it."

As the years went on, Gus and Anna brought in staff to help their sons, Jack and Frank, run the business. Jack remembers graduating high school

Gus Guerra purchased the Clover Leaf bar as a restarting point for his business, leaving Buddy's Rendezvous after selling it to friends James Bonacorsi and James Valente. *Guerra family*.

Gus Guerra often cooked at home for his family and employees, hosting business meetings in the kitchen as they enjoyed food and homemade wine. *Guerra family.*

and friends going to work for Chrysler and General Motors, getting the kind of engineering jobs he craved. Jack loved tearing engines apart and rebuilding them, so friends wanted him to join them in the engineering department. Jack knew he couldn't go.

"I couldn't do it because I had guilt. I had commitments here. I couldn't move on," Jack says. "Did I regret it? No, because I met a lot of really nice people here. It was a happy time."

Longtime staffers including Carol and Virginia "Ginny" Salci remember Gus and Anna as caring bosses. They'd test you to see if you were honest, Ginny recalls, but if you earned their trust, you had friends for life. Carol and Ginny, along with longtime employee Karen Magee DeFer, had young families when they joined the restaurant as waitresses or working behind the bar; soon enough, they became floor managers or kitchen managers. Other key employees were bartender Sharon "Granny" Augustine and Sally Mae Havrilla, who started as a cook and rose in the ranks. These women became like family, Marie says.

"The best was on Saturdays. They were all there. It was my favorite day," Karen Magee DeFer says. "People are usually afraid of their bosses. But I loved being around them as a family, all working together. Everybody had a part, and they all made it happen."

Best of all, Gus and Anna held staff meetings in their home, Ginny remembers, and they'd make everyone dinner as part of the deal. Anna would cook at the stove, stirring a pot of pasta or her homemade sauce while Gus grilled steaks in the fireplace. Everyone had a few glasses of Gus's homemade wine, and they talked about the business or just about anything at all, Carol and Ginny remember.

It had become a comfortable life—one that Gus never took for granted.

"My goal was to make the best Italian food possible and give people the best square pizza [around]," Gus said. "We've always felt that the type we make, a thick golden crust, is the best."

Chapter 5

BUDDY'S PIZZA

*A*ll businesses need a succession plan—a strategy to determine next steps for the company when the owners want to leave or something happens to them. The problem for James Valente and James Bonacorsi was how they would take their business partnership and translate it to the next generation. For these two men, who successfully ran Buddy's from the time they purchased it from Gus Guerra for a reported $33,000 in 1953, this felt like the one obstacle they couldn't resolve.

When Bonacorsi and Valente bought Buddy's, they came into the business as friends who shared common values. Their personalities helped define this era for the bar and pizzeria. Bonacorsi became known as Big Jimmy, a tribute to his broad chest, outgoing nature and grand ideas. Valente was dubbed Little Jimmy, a nod to his height, tailored presence and subtle approach to running the tavern side of the business. Big Jimmy had a work uniform of a white shirt, dress pants and, occasionally, an apron tied around his waist. Little Jimmy, with his perfectly pompadoured hair, always wore a suit and tie. Together, the two Jimmys were as familiar to Buddy's customers as the bocce ball court outside or the square pizza inside.

With their mutual commitment, they made Buddy's a destination restaurant. It was the right approach for the right time, as people in the 1950s were starting to eat out more, looking to give mom a break from nightly meal preparation and treat the kids to a new taste sensation known as pizza. During those boom years, Valente and Bonacorsi worked long hours, building up a staff of employees who helped seal Buddy's reputation for good food, quality service and being a comfortable place to socialize with card games, family gatherings and, of course, pizza.

But as they aged and started to think about retirement, one problem stood in their way: Who was going to get the restaurant? Big Jimmy wanted his portion of the partnership to go to his son. Little Jimmy wanted his share to go to his niece's husband. The debates about how to handle the transition ran longer and longer. By the time the two Jimmys were ready to move forward, it felt like their plans were doomed—Bonacorsi's son didn't necessarily want the restaurant, and Valente's nephew didn't necessarily want to work with Bonacorsi's son or have the funds to make the purchase happen.

How do you split up a business when you know it will also split up your families?

JAMES BONACORSI WAS BORN on March 30, 1909, in Mark, Illinois. His parents, Vincenzo and Giovanna (Bottino) Bonacorsi, were both born in Italy. Vincenzo arrived in the United States in 1902; Giovanna came two years later. They married in 1906 and had six children: Lino, James, Celia, Frank, August and Clotilde. August died in 1924 in a car accident.

For Vincenzo, working in an Illinois coal mine was better than starving back in his village, explained family historian Gary Bonacorsi. Gary says the mine advertised for workers in Italy, and the family came as part of a large influx of Italian immigrants into the United States. Many of their friends, including a couple named Paul and Maria Pina, settled into the Midwest. Tragedy struck in 1922 when Giovanna died of acute appendicitis. As the family's fortunes changed with the mine's shutdown, Vincenzo brought his family to Detroit.

"My grandfather Vincent didn't like the big city, so he returned to Illinois. Everyone else stayed," Gary says. "All five siblings stayed in Detroit. For the most part, everyone found a home, got married and started families....The whole family just knew how to work."

James served in the navy during World War II and had a series of jobs in automotive factories, including the assembly line at Chevrolet Gear and Axle at Holbrook and St. Aubin in Detroit, according to his draft card. He married Helen Holski in 1930, and they were soon ready to start a family. But one thing had to be settled first: Big Jimmy's life in the auto plants wasn't the right fit, family members say.

"My mom always said Jimmy was a real people person. You can't put him on an assembly line—he was too much of a people person," Gary says.

James Bonacorsi (*far left*) was one of five children, all of whom moved to Detroit to work at the auto plants or to own their own businesses. His siblings included Lino, Celia, Frank, August and Clotilde. *Bonacorsi family.*

Marie Guerra Easterby, Gus Guerra's daughter, says that according to family lore, Jimmy Bonacorsi was a friend and a customer at Buddy's when her father owned it. Marie says the Guerras and Bonacorsis were close enough that she called Big Jimmy's sister, Clotilde, by the affectionate nickname Aunt Babe.

Eugene Bonacorsi says his uncle Big Jimmy was unhappy at Chevrolet, and that resulted in his interest in owning something for himself. Another influence, Eugene says, was that his other brothers owned businesses as well.

"Jimmy ended up shopping around for a business and he ended up with Buddy's," Eugene Bonacorsi says.

Gary says Jimmy was a natural at the restaurant business, where service can be as important as the food. "They treated people so wonderfully. It wasn't a bar—it was an event," Gary says. "That's the best way to explain it. It was like *Cheers*, that television show. Everybody just hung out there. It was a family environment, and everybody had a wonderful time. The restaurant business was just built for him because he loved people."

Eugene Bonacorsi remembers his uncle working the restaurant floor like a pro. "Jimmy was always walking around, talking to the customers and going back into the kitchen to check on your pizzas," Eugene says.

Jimmy's escape from work was his Brighton cottage, Eugene and Gary recall. The little house on the lake gave Jimmy and Helen a place to entertain, and he always had a big smile on his face when he was there, Gary remembers. Jimmy and Helen's marriage was troubled by infertility, and their adoption of Thomas had eased that tension somewhat. However, Jimmy and Thomas had a strained relationship. So, having a place where they could get away, play cards, fish and go out on the pontoon was important, Eugene says.

"It wasn't anything real fancy; it was kinda homey-like. It was about the size of a garage and right on the water," Eugene says.

Both Eugene and Gary recall Jimmy going smelt fishing and returning with buckets of the small fish. Not only did he give away some of his catch to family, but he'd also bring some to Buddy's and host fish-fry events for the customers. "He'd come back with a pickup full of smelt. You'd bring a container, and he'd dip it into the smelt for you to take some home," Eugene says.

The only thing Eugene didn't like about his uncle was the pizza.

"I never used to like Uncle Jim's pizza for the fact that they put the tomato sauce on top," Eugene says. "They should have the sauce on the bottom where it belongs. I always thought that was the wrong way to make it."

JAMES "LITTLE JIMMY" VALENTE was born on October 1, 1913, in Clarksburg, West Virginia, to Bruno Valente and Mary Oliverio. He served a year in the army before he got married, getting hitched to Katherine in April 1946. He was thirty-two, and she was forty; it was her second marriage. By all accounts, theirs was a happy life.

Much like Big Jimmy, Little Jimmy was said to be eager to get out of the automotive plants. The two friends saved their money to make a down payment on Buddy's, and it was the break the duo had wanted for a long time, according to Little Jimmy's goddaughter, Kathy Jo Tourtois. Kathy Jo says Little Jimmy loved working in a bar because of the relaxed atmosphere and chances to socialize. Her family spent a lot of time at Buddy's as her father, Louis Tourtois, was a cook in the kitchen from about 1954 to 1970.

Little Jimmy lived up to his nickname in terms of his physical size compared to Bonacorsi, but he certainly was no wallflower, friends and associates say.

Louis Tourtois came to Detroit after calling his wife's uncle, James Valente, for a job. Valente, who co-owned Buddy's Pizza, invited him to work at the restaurant. *Tourtois family.*

"He always wanted to be a big shot," Kathy Jo says. She remembers him chomping on cigars and keeping the waitstaff running if they dared to slow down and his sense of humor—all key parts of Little Jimmy's personality.

Those signature cigars are also how Richard Sosin remembers Little Jimmy. Sosin got to know both Big Jimmy and Little Jimmy when they were members of the John W. Smith Old Timers Club, a social group for people who own bars or taverns around Metro Detroit. The Jimmys became members when they bought Buddy's, Sosin says, and they were beloved members of the group, which also raised funds for charities. Sosin's father was a member of the Old Timers Club, and that is how he got to know the two.

"[Valente] looked like Groucho Marx—he was short and always had a cigar in his mouth," Sosin recalls. "Both Jimmys worked for Ford and were friends with Gus [Guerra] when they bought Buddy's....They were two nice guys, with good marriages and nice wives."

Little Jimmy also loved the nightlife, going out with anyone who wanted to join him after work. Little Jimmy was beloved within Buddy's, as well, because he took the time to celebrate with the staff, taking the entire crew to Mario's on Second for dinner and then Elmwood Casino for a nightclub show, says Skip McClatchey, who worked at Buddy's as a busboy.

Pierino "Pete" Piccinato, Connie's son, says he also remembers the trips to Canada with fondness. Pete says it was like a huge family outing with the Buddy's staff. A favorite spot was Windsor's first casino, the Elmwood Hotel and Supper Club on the city's southwest side. According to lore, many top musical acts performed there, including Ella Fitzgerald and Jimmy Durante.

"Once a year, he'd take everyone to [Elmwood] casino to see the nightclub acts. We'd all have dinner and see the show," Pete says.

Kathy Jo remembers those same trips to Mario's for Italian food as well as trips into Canada to the Top Hat. They'd go as big groups, traveling to see bands like the Gold Diggers, which fascinated Kathy Jo. Little Jimmy even took the family on vacations, traveling back home as well as to more exotic locations like Las Vegas.

Little Jimmy had a reputation for being a good, lifelong friend. Many agree his temperament was an ideal balance to chef Louis Tourtois. The Frenchman often lost his temper when he was upset with the way things were being done in the kitchen or the level of quality within the recipes he passionately protected. Little Jimmy could smooth things over while also helping Louis make amends as needed.

"Big Jimmy and Little Jimmy were bigger than life," recalls Wes Pikula, whose mother worked at Buddy's and who has been with the pizza company himself since he was a high school student.

BUDDY'S RESTAURANT IN THE "Two Jimmy" years was fulfilling in the best kinds of ways, says Skip McClatchey. McClatchey's father got his job there because he knew Big Jimmy; he was working as a bartender to make ends meet for his family of ten children. The Jimmys knew how to make the work fun, Skip says. For example, they'd dye the mostaccioli green in honor of his father, whose birthday was close to St. Patrick's Day.

Skip says the Six Mile restaurant had a tight group working on the restaurant floor. They'd commute together, eat together, hang out after work and take care of one another. Some of his favorites included Yvonne, a waitress who had to have everything "look just perfect," Skip says.

"We worked hard, and we enjoyed ourselves," Skip says. "Everybody had family or friends working there. The idea of that is very smart—if you have good workers, they'll bring other good workers. And you'll make sure they

Buddy's "Supreme Court" included Anna, Connie, Louisa, Dee, Sabina and Mary, all of whom ran Buddy's like their own. *Buddy's Pizza.*

work hard because you don't want to be embarrassed by them....If you worked hard together, it was a little bit easier for everybody."

Big Jimmy also had a strong viewpoint about the kind of people he wanted to serve, Skip says. "When you're behind that bar, these are not customers. You make them friends. If you make friends, you never have to worry about that cash register. That was his work philosophy—you treat everyone there as a friend," Skip says.

Skip has particularly fond memories of Connie Piccinato, whom he describes as a mom type who knew everything about Buddy's and was always helping the crew. Connie was in charge of the salad station, and her salad dressing was the reason people came back to Buddy's so often for the pizza and salad, Skip says.

"She would do anything for the customers. They were like friends and family," Skip says. "With her salad, everything had to be fresh and done by hand. She'd break up the lettuce by hand and get it down to bite-sized pieces. Then she'd add the dressing. Then the ham, cheese, salami and tomatoes. She had her way of doing it, and it worked perfectly."

While the salad dressing was her recipe and her top secret, the crew knew its basics, Skip says.

"She made it in front of everybody," Skip says. "She'd line up these gallon jugs, add a little bit of salt, pepper, oregano, cut-up lemons, onion, celery. Then she'd add just so much vinegar and oil....She'd put it down in the cooler and let it marinate. She kept track of everything and when it could be used."

The pizza recipe was also closely guarded, Skip says. But, once again, everyone knew a little bit about everything.

"All of the recipes were very basic—flour, water, yeast and salt. You just kind of do it to where it's just right," Skip says. "You have to get the texture of the dough just right, then you have to start making the balls. Then, you have to stretch it and stretch it again. It takes work, but it's really not a secret. It's just not many people want to do that much work."

Lots of people did try to learn the recipes, Skip says. But how they went about it was the tougher part.

"There were two Eds who ran Mr. Eds, and one of them lived next door to Connie. People said Connie must have given him the recipe for the pizza," Skip says. "But he swore that he figured out how to make the pizza by going through the dumpster to get all of the ingredients."

Skip says Big Jimmy was the one who took care of the bocce ball court, getting it ready every spring for the men who played there. "He'd even it out, roll it and sprinkle it so it wouldn't get too dusty. You had to do that regularly because [Big Jimmy] didn't want the dust to bother the customers eating out there," Skip says.

According to a *Detroit News* interview, Bonacorsi became an authority on bocce when he worked in the coal-mining camps back in Illinois. "We used to play between shifts," Bonacorsi told the newspaper in 1975. "I remember those days well. The camps were full of Italian workers, and all we had for entertainment was a small tavern, a soccer ball and boccie. It kept your mind off the back-breaking work and was a great outlet for emotions."

Big Jimmy told the *News* in a 1968 interview that these boccie and card players were responsible for Buddy's success. "Senior citizens made this place. It's like a club for them," he said. They played games like Scopa, Briscola and

Generations of people enjoyed a game of bocce and a boomba (a large serving of beer) at the court at Buddy's Pizzeria at Six Mile and Conant. *Buddy's Pizza.*

Tres Siete while drinking beer or Coffee Royal (a mix of black coffee, a teaspoon of sugar and a shot of whiskey).

Next door to the bocce court was a room where people sat and played cards, Skip says. "Three Finger Frank, Shorty— these guys came every day. It was like a social club for them. They drank coffee or little bottles of beer. They would play cards for who was buying the next round. They were always there."

According to family lore, the two Jimmys were ready to retire around 1969 or early 1970. Another version of the story has it they weren't getting along as well by then, and they put the place up for sale. Valente was around fifty-six, and Bonacorsi was sixty. Depending on who you ask, the Jimmys agreed to split the business in half, one part going to Bonacorsi's son, Thomas, and the other half going to Valente's nephew by marriage, Louis Tourtois. However, Thomas liked working in the kitchen, but he had no interest in owning or running Buddy's, which complicated the whole situation.

"Big Jimmy and Little Jimmy decided to retire. Big Jimmy's son and Louis were going to run the business. But the two didn't get along," Skip recalls. "They weren't going to run it right, the Jimmys thought, so they decided to sell it and wash their hands of it. Louis stayed on and worked for the new group that bought it, but then he decided to go out on his own."

Valente and Bonacorsi finally got an outside offer and decided to accept it. The couple that made them such a sweet deal? Two people you'd never think would want to get into the restaurant business: Southfield-based entrepreneurs William and Shirlee Jacobs.

WILLIAM AND SHIRLEE JACOBS had never worked in hospitality, a bar or a restaurant—or anywhere near one. William, who went by the nickname Billy, was in real estate. Shirlee Sklare worked as an interior decorator, coming from a family well known within the drapery industry. The couple married in 1946 in a candlelight ceremony at the Statler Hotel.

Billy was born in New Jersey, and his family moved to Michigan when he was a kid. Friends recalled the financial insecurity of their childhood years, when they mostly played outside for lack of funds to do anything else. "We couldn't afford a football or a basketball, so we played kick the can all of the time," childhood friend Harold Haas told the *Jewish News*. Billy graduated from Northern High School in Detroit and enlisted in the U.S. Army. He served as a second lieutenant in World War II, winning a Bronze Star for saving a soldier's life. Billy returned to Detroit, where he attended Wayne State University. He got into real estate, owning a variety of properties from motels to nursing homes to shopping centers.

Robert says his parents went to Buddy's for the first time with some family friends. After that visit, the couple ate at the restaurant frequently. It was Shirlee's idea to make an offer on Buddy's to Valente and Bonacorsi. While Billy is said to have felt mystified about why his wife wanted the business, they purchased it anyway.

Initially, Billy Jacobs was going to be just the investor, and his partners were going to run the place. According to Michigan's liquor license transfer records, Buddy's went from James Bonacorsi and Katherine Valente to William Jacobs, Max Waxer and Allan A. Rotman in June 1970. According to a *Crain's Detroit* interview by freelance reporter Lawrence Paladino, Billy said that deal soon fell apart, and he had to buy them out. Now, the question became who was going to operate Buddy's from day to day.

"It was easy in a sense because we had a name—we were the pizza that won the contest in the *Detroit News*. The business was a very flourishing business and everybody knew their own job. We had good people," Billy Jacobs told Paladino.

Billy was a quieter type, and Shirlee did most of the talking—something that offered a balance in the relationship and set up their roles at Buddy's. What was going to initially be "just a hobby" or "a kibbitz for his wife," as Billy told Paladino, started to become a time-consuming yet profitable place to operate.

"What I learned from my father was watching what he did," Robert says. "My father was a quiet man, but he also was a very smart guy....My mother more than made up for it, I'll tell you that. In my family, my mother was more difficult and the talker."

Billy set the tone of how the Jacobs family would operate Buddy's early on for Robert, he says.

"I was more mathematic about it, always asking how can we save on cost," Robert says. "My father saw me thinking this way, and he told me, 'Listen, Robert, we're always trying to improve the quality. We're not looking to save some money.' It's easy to make mistakes. If I didn't listen to my dad,

William and Shirlee Jacobs purchased Buddy's Pizza from James Valente and James Bonacorsi with partners; they eventually ran the business with their son, Robert. *Buddy's Pizza.*

who had more business experience, I would have tried to save $3 on a case of mushrooms if it would have tasted just as good. But my father said, 'No, we're not doing that.'"

Buddy's legacy is the Jacobs legacy, Robert said. When Billy Jacobs died in December 2001, the Buddy's Pizza marquees at its then nine locations displayed messages such as, "We'll miss you, Billy."

SHIRLEE PUT IN HER hours at the restaurant at first, but she soon gave that up and turned things over to Buddy's longtime staff, Robert says. Robert attended Southfield High School and graduated from Wayne State University's law school. While there, he worked part time at Buddy's as a bartender—likely one of the worst the restaurant ever had, Robert says. He formally joined Buddy's full time around 1975.

"My father needed someone to run Buddy's, so after law school, I got more involved," Robert says. "At that point, I was really managing Buddy's for my folks. There was also a manager over the staff."

The one thing they all agreed on was the potential Buddy's had for expansion, looking to how they could grow the business to other locations. Growth came slowly, with carryout locations and then full-fledged restaurants. Expansion was a challenge, Robert says, but a necessary one to scale buying and marketing.

"We didn't want to open up that many restaurants. We wanted to be really conservative, making sure the quality was there," Robert says. "We always felt our reputation was at stake."

Buddy's opened additional locations in Livonia and Waterford in the early 1980s. Its key strategy was to set up in locations with automotive facilities nearby, banking on hungry autoworkers and automotive executives. Buddy's couldn't be Domino's or Little Caesars—but it could be successful at what it did best, which was square pizza.

Another key acquisition around this time was the addition of Wesley "Wes" Pikula to the Buddy's executive team. Pikula's mother had worked at the Six and Conant Buddy's location, and he joined as well, as a dishwasher and busboy. Robert says he soon came to rely on Wes.

"The fact that we were on the same page makes a lot of difference. He had the obsession. I had the obsession, too," Robert says. "Our obsession

Wes Pikula (*second row, second from left*) joined Buddy's in 1975 after his mother worked there. He worked closely with Irv Sosnick (*top row, far left*), one of the restaurant's longtime managers. *Buddy's Pizza.*

was making a great, consistent product. We complemented each other. And that doesn't come easy.

"At the end of the day, I was fortunate enough to have great people around me. If you don't have great people executing, the product goes downhill very quickly. I was very lucky to have Wesley and a few other people who really had the same care and love and passion and also brains."

Just like his father, Robert says he wants Buddy's to be the best at what it does, and that's serve Detroit Style pizza.

"I still care. I can assure you I still care. This is essentially my legacy," Robert says.

WES PIKULA'S FAMILY MOVED to Detroit around 1973, and he says he first showed up on his bike outside of Buddy's with a group of friends, all looking for work.

"I found out they didn't need any dishwashers, but a few weeks later, I heard there was an opening. The manager Cass called me and asked if I wanted a job, and I started on first shift on a Friday night," Wes says. "It was horrible. The place was open until 1:30 a.m., but you didn't get out until 3:00 a.m. I had to walk home from there. I'd be soaking wet because they didn't have plastic aprons and I had to wear a regular cloth apron."

Thankfully, Wes says he was moved up to busboy and started helping out in the kitchen. He learned the ropes of grinding the cheese, chopping the lettuce and stretching the dough, he says. He graduated from Hamtramck St. Ladislaus in 1976 and was attending Wayne State University when he started learning every role within Buddy's, including bartender. When he graduated from WSU in 1981, Wes was hoping to get a job in his chosen field. "I loved Buddy's, but I went to school to work in marketing and finance," Wes says.

As fate would have it, Wes's timing was poor. The nation had soaring gas prices and high inflation. Wes was ready to find his first job, but the economy had gone south. The best gig he says he could find was in the mailroom at Campbell Ewald, an advertising agency.

Around this time, the Jacobs family came to Wes and suggested he stay on with Buddy's in a different capacity. They were looking for managers to help with the expansion, and they asked Wes to help them open up the Farmington Hills location. Wes would establish the process for opening new restaurants and a set standard of procedures for employees to follow, both at Six and Conant and its other sites. By 1983, Wes was helping open up other Buddy's locations, including one in Livonia, where he was the manager.

"I moved from the manager to executive general manager to vice president of operations," Wes says. "I've been involved in all phases of the business, from setting up training manuals to design to working on the marketing side, making sure that Buddy's was always at the forefront of restaurant operations."

While Wes says Robert wanted to emulate successful chains like Chuck Muir's spots, Wes wanted the Jacobs family to maintain the traditions and recipes that had made Buddy's what it was, including honoring the original creator, Gus Guerra.

"This was a labor of love for many people," Wes says. "When they bought Buddy's, there was a staff here that maintained it. With pizza, you have to manage it every day. If you're passionate about the product, you'll maintain the product. If you're sloppy, the pizza doesn't come out right.... [The recipe] was sacred. It was like the Holy Grail. You didn't question or touch anything."

By the time the economy recovered, Wes wanted to stay. He knew he had found his life's work.

"The love people have for Buddy's made me fall in love with it," Wes says. "That made me work even harder to fulfill that expectation."

Chapter 6

SHIELD'S/LOUI'S PIZZA

*F*or Louis Tourtois, the short walk from his home to Shield's Bar was a daily reminder of what he had gained and what he had lost. Working in Shield's tiny kitchen was hardly glamorous. There was barely enough room to sling the dough. But it served its purpose—it got him away from Buddy's and out on his own.

At Shield's, Louis could run his side of the business the way he wanted. He had honed his craft at Buddy's, where he had worked since he was a teenager. But he also had tricks of his own, never divulging the secrets he knew about that sacred recipe. At Shield's, the money was split: the owners kept the bar tabs, and Louis kept the pizzeria receipts. His partner, Annie Babinski, helped him along with his son, Louis Tourtois Jr. Although he wasn't a classically trained chef, Louis liked having his own space, keeping the kitchen the way he wanted it and prepping everything with his own hands.

Lines of customers following Louis from Buddy's to Shield's kept the place busy. But it also made Shield's owners jealous. Louis had a temper, and they had clashed more than a few times. According to Louis's family, the first shock came when the Polish brothers who owned Shield's sold the place in 1974 to a Greek immigrant named Constantine "Deano" Moraitis. Louis felt they should have offered Shield's to him. Despite this rift, the chef and Deano kept working together, perhaps because of Deano's keen interest in how the kitchen was run.

The second shock came about two years later. It started like any other day: Louis and the regular crew arrived to work, ready for another long

Louis Tourtois worked as a pizza maker at Buddy's before leaving in 1970 to work at Shield's, a small bar located down the street from Buddy's. Annie Babinski (*left*) was one of his business partners and James Valente's stepdaughter. *Tourtois family.*

shift. With no warning, Deano confronted Louis and told him to get out, the chef's family says. Louis got his son, and they started moving their gear out of the kitchen. On one of their return trips, Louis tried one of the doors to the kitchen, which was normally kept open. To his surprise, it was locked. He tried the other—same.

Louis only had keys to these two doors, so he tried to fit them into the locks. No luck. Louis probably gave his key a little shake, trying to twist it this way and that. No dice.

What happened, according to Louis's grandson Nykolas Sulkiwskyj, was that Deano likely changed the locks the day before without telling Louis. According to pizza lore, Deano had found a way to get Tourtois's pizza recipe and didn't need the man who created it anymore.

"My dad had no clue," says Kathy Jo Tourtois, Louis's daughter. "Deano tossed dad out."

LOUIS EDMOND TOURTOIS WAS born on May 21, 1936, in France. He was raised in Hericourt, just on the other side of the Swiss border in a picturesque part of the country. His childhood was blown apart by the German invasion in World War II. The Tourtois family tried to survive amid the chaos of war, but when limited food supplies led them to starvation, his family had to evacuate. According to family lore, Louis's sister was killed in that escape, stabbed by a German soldier. Nykolas said his grandfather never spoke of what he saw or experienced and likely had PTSD from it. "He'd start shaking if you even mentioned it," Nykolas says.

Louis recounted his childhood to *Detroit News* reporter Jim Treloar. "Ever go four-five days without eating? Your belly swells from the hunger. I don't know what you call it here, but in France, we called it, 'the carrot.' When my mother couldn't cope any longer, she sent us to live with my grandparents. Grandpa was a hunter. He shot anything that moved—rabbits, blue jays, crows. Pretty soon, there were no more birds around Hericourt. Don't laugh; crow makes a hell of a soup. When a bomb fell and killed a horse or cow, grandpa ran for it with his butcher knife. They didn't stay dead very long. I'll tell you that. I know what dog tastes like, and cat. It's a hell of a thing, being hungry. Maybe that's why I went into the food business."

Louis's mother met and married an Italian American soldier, and the family moved to the United States around 1948. They settled in his hometown of Clarksburg, West Virginia, a little city with a large Italian population. Louis's mother was a self-taught cook, Kathy Jo Tourtois says, creating gourmet meals and cranking out enough cakes to become a well-known baker and wedding cake designer.

Around age fifteen, Louis met Katherine Joan Valente at school. Louis was trying to learn English quickly, Kathy Jo says, and Katherine took him on as a pet project. The two teens fell in love, and as was the custom of the times, got married. Both made it through eleventh grade, Kathy Jo says. Louis took a job working as a bricklayer in Youngstown, Ohio, to support their little family, but frequent layoffs had him looking for steadier work.

That's when Louis called on his new wife's uncle, a doting character who was said to have recently purchased a bar and pizzeria in Detroit. James Valente was his niece's favorite, and Valente told Louis to bring the family up to Detroit—he'd make sure the Frenchman would find work at Buddy's Rendezvous. Louis learned the basic recipe from a legendary Buddy's cook named Dominick. Eventually, Nykolas says, Louis began working his way up through the kitchen to become its top pizza chef and the restaurant's manager.

Louis Tourtois and his wife, Katherine, met and married when they were teenagers in West Virginia. She taught him how to speak English after he moved to the United States from France. *Tourtois family*.

Part of what made Louis a force in the kitchen was his size and stamina. He was of average height, but he stayed in shape from his younger years as a boxer and track runner, Nykolas said. He also retained much of his French accent. Many servers, bussers and line cooks recall that accent growing whenever Tourtois got irritated—which, it turns out, was often.

Louis ran the kitchen in such a way that everyone who worked with him knew he was the boss, says Skip McClatchey, who worked at Buddy's for about ten years before starting his own restaurant in the area, Sabina's.

"He could get real hot. But he was real fair, too," Skip says. "He would get hot in the moment. If it was a busy day, he wanted everything to go just right. He was a real stickler for quality. With pizza, you have to be real careful. If you bang it on the table, it will go flat. You have to treat the dough carefully. It was all about quality. But as long as you worked hard, by the end of the day, everything was fine. He yelled at you in the middle. I never took it badly."

As the story goes, James "Jimmy" Valente had a partnership with James "Jimmy" Bonacorsi in which, in the event they were to sell Buddy's to a new owner, both of their equal shares would go to a person of their choosing. Bonacorsi was supposed to sell his portion to his adopted son. Valente would sell his share of the business to Louis. When the time came to sell, however, either Bonacorsi's son wasn't interested or Tourtois didn't have the funds to make his portion of the sale possible. As a result, the deal with both partners failed, and Tourtois was out of the running to purchase the business. Instead, the two Jimmys sold the restaurant to the Jacobs family for what Nykolas called "an offer they couldn't refuse."

"They didn't give it to my grandfather, straight up," Nykolas says. "It was going to be a partnership or we're going to give it to someone else."

Louis, at that point, had worked at Buddy's for about seventeen years. According to Wes Pikula: "Louis stayed on, hoping to buy the place at the time. But he didn't have any money; he was just working in the kitchen."

Another source of umbrage came shortly thereafter when, in 1970, the *Detroit News* announced its now-infamous pizza contest. According to lore, Louis created the square pizza that Buddy's entered in the newspaper's contest. He made it the morning of the judging, preparing it with Buddy's

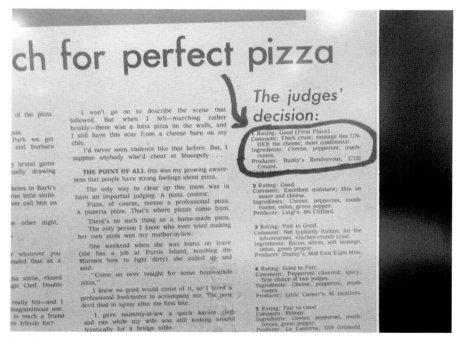

Buddy's Pizza was proud to be named the top pizza in Detroit by the *Detroit News*, but a manager crossed out Louis Tourtois's name from the article, which hangs in Buddy's to this day. *Author's collection.*

ingredients but in his own home. Louis took his creation to the *Detroit News* for the tasting. Buddy's came in first place and the article about the contest credits Louis Tourtois as the cook.

After Buddy's won that contest, Nykolas said the owners painted a blue ribbon on the building as a symbol of victory. But they forgot one person in that process—their chef. When you look at the copy of that article hanging in Buddy's restaurant today, Nykolas says, you'll see Louis's name is crossed out.

One of Buddy's longtime managers, Irv Sosnick, did the honors with a thick black pen, to note that Buddy's should have been listed as the pizza's creator rather than an individual chef, Wes Pikula says.

WHEN TOURTOIS STARTED LOOKING for his next restaurant, he didn't have to go far. Shield's Bar was less than half a mile down the road from Buddy's and a few blocks away from where Tourtois was living at the time. At that point, the bar served limited food—maybe some fish and chips on a Friday, Nykolas said. The owners, two Polish guys, worked out a handshake deal with the French pizza maker. They'd get the bar's take, and Tourtois would get all the money from the kitchen. They brought in ovens and told Tourtois to get to work.

"Just like with the Jimmys, they promised the place to Louis," Nykolas says. "The theme of this is broken promises."

Crowds began to form at Shield's Bar when regulars realized the guy who made the pizzas they had enjoyed at Buddy's had moved down the street. Louis made it a family affair with his son, Louis Tourtois or "Junior," starting work as a busboy and dishwasher around age nine. By the time Junior was thirteen, Louis had taught him how to mix dough.

The pizza at Shield's was a standout, recalled James Simokovich, who was a busboy and kitchen helper when he was a teenager at Buddy's Pizza in the mid-1970s. He remembers eating at all three restaurants when Tourtois was the main pizza chef—Buddy's, Shield's and, later, Loui's Pizza.

"I don't think anything can come close to the way Mr. Tourtois did his pizzas," Simokovich says. As far as the recipes go, "He didn't share anything with anybody."

Louis had the Shield's operation humming.

"Louis was making so much money from the kitchen," Skip McClatchy says. "More people were coming in for the food than were coming in for the bar."

Louis didn't know that there were forces at work. Deano Moraitis had gone to the two Polish brothers with a deal. According to the Tourtois family, the brothers were looking to retire, and none of their kids wanted to take over the business. Once again, someone made an offer, and the owner accepted it without telling Louis what had happened. Seven years of a partnership that had made both sides a goodly amount of money was over.

Then came the locked door. That meant only one thing, Nykolas says: Louis felt he had been betrayed, again.

"That's when my grandfather said he was done working for people," Nykolas recalls. "He said he was going to open his own place."

LOUIS STARTED WITH GRAND plans—believe it or not, Nykolas says there was a French bistro between Shield's and his own pizza place. But that kind of fine dining didn't work out. Louis went back to what he knew best. In 1976, he bought an old restaurant in Hazel Park once known as D'Angelos. It was a classic Italian restaurant that served a little bit of everything, from steak to pasta to pizza. As the story goes, Louis decided to call the place Loui's because another place already had Louis's Pizza as its name. Plus, it sounded fancier, Kathy Jo says.

Louis told *Detroit News* reporter Jim Treloar that the order of ingredients was key to his pizza. The pepperoni had to go under the cheese so it wouldn't burn as it cooked. The cheese had to be brick for its butterfat content, which could stand up to the oven's high heat.

"In the oven, that cheese spreads out across the pizza, and when it hits the side of the hot pan, it toasts," Louis told the reporter. "And it forms a little ridge of toasted cheese all along the edge of the pizza. Some folks think that's the best part. I've seen 'em when they've eaten all the pizza they can, but they'll sit there, picking away at that toast cheese 'til there's nothing left. Then the vegetables...and the sauce last. That way, the vegetables get marinated and cooked in the sauce as it seeps down through each layer."

Louis rarely talked about his early days at Buddy's, Nykolas says. "As soon as I started coming around, you couldn't even mention the name Buddy's to my grandpa. He's start cussing up a storm," Nykolas says. "My grandpa was so bitter because he always knew Buddy's was supposed to be his. He knew damn well he eventually would buy out little Bonacorsi because Junior [Jimmy Bonacorsi's son] was lazy. He had his own pizza, and for two or three years, when he ran out, he wouldn't make more dough."

Competitors also could be friends; Louis Tourtois (*middle*) worked with Jimmy Bonacorsi (*far right*) during a charity event. *Tourtois family*.

By 1978, the pizza wars that started the moment Gus Guerra moved to East Detroit had escalated. It was Buddy's versus Cloverleaf versus Loui's, going for the throats of their competitors. They slung mud in the newspapers whenever they were interviewed.

"We've got cooks here who can tear a pizza apart and analyze every ingredient in it," Robert Jacobs, Buddy's co-owner, told Laura Berman of the *Detroit Free Press* that July. "We've eaten Loui's pizza, sure. It's good, very good, but then so is ours."

Louis slapped back. "I am never satisfied," he told the *Freep*. "I am always making changes, making my pizza better. Pizza has changed a lot since I first learned how to make it….Some people are good writers. Some people are good at drawing or at being doctors. I make good pizza."

Even Robert had to agree in that same article: "I'll be really honest. A few years ago, when Louis was making pizza at Shield's, his was better than ours. We had some people managing Buddy's who let the quality slip."

One familiar face from Buddy's came with Louis to his new pizzeria: James "Little Jimmy" Valente. Dressed in a good suit with his hair groomed perfectly, Little Jimmy showed up to Loui's every day as a kind of host for the place. Also known as "Uncle Jim," Valente seated people, chatted up the customers and helped out when needed. If you didn't find him in the kitchen, you'd likely see him sitting at the bar, having a good time with friends.

Little Jimmy told the *Freep* he took the job "for the exercise. I am retired." But that was hardly the case, Kathy Jo says. He loved when people mistook him for the chef or owner. But on those rare occasions when a customer was upset, Kathy Jo says Little Jimmy identified himself as only the host and sent the person directly to Louis to complain.

Part of the reason the Valente and the Tourtois families stayed close was that they were neighbors as well. Valente had lived in Detroit for decades, but Louis talked him into moving to the suburbs when his house was burglarized. Everyone lived in the same neighborhood. Nykolas said he recalled going from house to house when he was a kid, stopping in to see his grandfather as a daily habit.

As AN OLD-SCHOOL PIZZA maker, Louis liked to keep things simple, Nykolas says. The pizza had pepperoni, mushrooms and onion, and that's it.

"Some people started bringing in little baggies of vegetables, like green peppers. So, my grandpa finally said he might as well get all of that stuff and offer it on the pizzas," Nykolas says. "He also didn't want to bring in cheese sticks on the menu because he wanted people to enjoy the pizza and the antipasto. But they end up ordering all three."

When he served the pizza, Louis told the *Detroit News* he also liked to double the sauce. "The extra sauce makes it a little juicer, and I like that," the chef told Jim Treloar.

Veteran waitresses who worked with Tourtois at Buddy's and then Shield's ended up following the family again to Hazel Park. These loyal longtimers helped serve customers and give Loui's a reputation for feeding families and hosting parties with spirit and service. Louis asked Annie to be his partner at Loui's, but she declined and instead worked there at the register for many years, Kathy Jo says.

"They knew what it was. They knew he wasn't messing around. They knew he was serious," Nykolas says.

Although the bar was always a prime spot in the dining room to sit and shoot the breeze, drinks were well and good, Louis used to say—but Loui's was first and foremost a pizzeria. The food had to be the star.

"We're a restaurant first before we're a bar. The drinks come second. They make you more of a profit, but we wanted quality over quantity," Nykolas says. "You can get drinks anywhere. You get more loyal clients with good

Family often worked closely together at Detroit's early pizzerias, including Katherine Tourtois at Loui's Pizzeria in Hazel Park. *Tourtois family.*

food. [My grandpa] always said it had to be the right way or no way at all.… Everything we do here is by hand. We don't weigh anything. Everything is eyeballed, like art."

The décor was pure Louis, as well. He put in crushed red velvet booths, a dramatic, dark ceiling that sparkled like stars and his own paintings on the walls. Louis was a big Bob Ross fan and painted in his spare time for relaxation, Nykolas says. After falling in love with a restaurant on vacation that hung chianti bottles from the walls and ceiling, he started the tradition at Loui's, as well.

"It's not even a Detroit thing," Nykolas says. "We used to have more wine bottles, but their weight caved in a wall."

Louis told Molly Abraham of the *Detroit News* that he liked when people autographed the bottles he then hung on the restaurant's walls. "People like to feel they belong, and this helps give them that feeling," he said.

NYKOLAS STARTED AT THE pizzeria when he was a teenager, learning the ropes from the old-timers and studying his grandfather's original recipes. It was a point of family pride that the third generation was running the business.

There was a time when the second generation was in charge, Nykolas says, but illness made it hard for his uncle, Louis Tourtois II, to run Loui's the way he wanted to do it. He stepped back, so someone had to step up.

"I did dough every summer from when I was thirteen years old," Nykolas says. "I played football, and when I wasn't playing, I was here. I graduated in 2013 and ended up coaching middle school football for a year. I was up north when I found out my grandpa had a massive heart attack and I realized I've got to be the one to do this now. My uncle and cousin were supposed to take it over, but my cousin ended up with brain cancer and passed away. My uncle…couldn't handle employees anymore.

"It was either you want it and you take it or we're losing Loui's," Nykolas says. "My grandpa put in forty years. He didn't put in forty years for nothing. I'm going to do it. It's all-important to me—food and family."

Chapter 7

THE GREAT PIZZA DEBATE

*I*n Detroit, one singular year came to define the who's who of pizza. In 1970, the *Detroit News* ran an article about which pizzeria had the best pie, using the results of a pizza-eating event held in the newsroom. While the contest was hastily organized and decidedly unscientific, the ramifications of its winning proclamation echoed across the local industry for decades to follow.

Titled "The Great Pizza Debate," James Treloar's article ran in the Kitchen Talk section of the *Detroit News* on Wednesday, July 15, 1970. The article filled the front page of the food section that day. Granted, it was section E, so it likely took a lot of digging through the paper to find it. But its headline was almost as large as the section title.

The article is simple in concept: Treloar tells the story of his family's personal experiences with pizza. He goes over his family's debates over who makes the best pizza; his teen son, David, claims it is Giordano's. Treloar himself declares it is Magic Chef. Some local friends say it is Bon Fiesta.

This is where Treloar says he came up with the idea to have a pizza contest, inviting seven of Detroit's professional pizza makers to submit entries. His only criteria were that the pizza had to be off the menu, "nothing fancy-shmancy" and something the public could buy. He got eleven of the newspaper's "most ardent pizza enthusiasts" to serve as the judges; one famous member was Molly Abraham, who later became a noted food reviewer for that newspaper and others. The *Detroit News* published the results, ranking the pizzas from first to last. The photo accompanying

The *Detroit News* pizza contest caused years of dissent between the main Detroit Style pizza people and companies, including Buddy's and Louis Tourtois, its former pizza maker. *Author's collection.*

the article told a story of its own, with six round pies creating a circle around the winner: the square pizza from Buddy's Rendezvous at Six and Conant in Detroit.

The judges ranked Buddy's as "good," earning first place. The comments on the pizza read as follows: "Thick crust; sausage lies UNDER the cheese; most continental." The cook is listed as Louis Tourtois.

You'd think that would be the end of it. But, indeed, pizzerias still talk about this article with a mix of spite and despair.

FOR BUDDY'S, THE CONTEST and resulting article created a mix of pride and disquiet about who actually made the pizza. For Cloverleaf, the contest was seen as unfair not only because of who was allowed to compete but also because it was a breaking point that severed business ties in a way that resonates across the decades. For the Treloar family, the contest created a secret that took years to surface and caused considerable consternation, says Tim Treloar, son of the Pulitzer Prize–winning journalist.

Buddy's immediately capitalized on the contest's results. The owners painted a giant blue ribbon on the building's exterior, extoling its pizza as the No. 1 pie in the city. Other accolades would follow, but this kind of advertising was key to Buddy's stepping up as the best in the city, says Wes Pikula.

"Every business [in Detroit] had to submit their pizza, and every business had its name under its pizza," Pikula recalls. "When it went to Buddy's [as the winner], it made Buddy's the story in that area."

The debate at Buddy's became about who got credit for that No. 1 pizza pie. Tourtois was at odds with the Jacobs family, who now owned Buddy's, and the French chef was preparing to go to Shield's. The Tourtois family emphasizes his impact of the Buddy's pizza winning the contest.

"My dad cooked the pizza at home in their oven on Eureka in Detroit," says Kathy Jo Tourtois, Louis's daughter. "He wasn't going to do it, but my mom talked him into it. So, he made the pizza at home. That's why my dad was always so upset with the contest. 'Everyone thinks it was Buddy's, not me,' he'd say."

Indeed, Wes questions whether Louis Tourtois should get the credit for making the pizza because it was Buddy's recipe.

"He left here. After they had the pizza contest in 1970, Louis left shortly thereafter," Wes says. "It went to Buddy's. Louis put his name underneath the thing. It was a Buddy's pizza he made.…Louis Junior was a friend of mine. We grew up in the same neighborhood. His sister gets all worked up

Buddy's Pizza painted a large no. 1 ribbon on its exterior after winning the first place slot in the 1970 *Detroit News* pizza contest. *Author's collection.*

Louis Tourtois had his own ribbon added to his sign at Loui's Pizzeria in Hazel Park, which he opened on his own in the late 1970s. *Author's collection.*

about it because Louis made the pizza at home. He had to because you had to have the pizza to the *Detroit News* in the morning, so Louis took the ingredients home and made it there. 'It was my dad's,' they say. But that's because Buddy's wasn't open at the time."

Incidentally, if you look at the Loui's Pizza sign in Hazel Park, you'll notice a ribbon on that sign, as well. It's basically a subtle slap at Buddy's for the over-the-top ribbon on its building—and it includes the year 1954, when Louis Tourtois started making Detroit Style pie, Kathy Jo says.

Meanwhile, Cloverleaf co-owner Jack Guerra says he felt the *Detroit News* unfairly excluded his family's pizza from the contest. Guerra says his dad; his brother, Frank; and the family's attorney all contacted the newspaper through mail and telephone calls, imploring them to include Cloverleaf. After all, Gus Guerra had created the original Detroit pizza at Buddy's.

However, the *Detroit News* would not relent in its decision that the pizzerias allowed to enter had to be in Detroit proper. Gus owned a pizzeria in East Detroit (now known as Eastpointe), and that disqualified Cloverleaf from participating, Jack Guerra says.

"We had a good pizza, and we thought we had a good shot at it. My father called about it. My brother called about it. They told them that you were excluded, you can't enter the contest, because you're not inside Detroit city limits," Jack Guerra says. "Our bookkeeper's son, Max, was a prosecuting attorney, and he wrote a letter to the *Detroit News* as well. But they told us, 'Tough shit.…You're not in Detroit. You can't be in the contest.'

"There were a lot of good pizza companies around at the time. How come nobody else can get in?" Guerra says. "Buddy's took first place, and that hurt us, I know that. But there was nothing we could do about it."

TIM TRELOAR SAYS HIS father was a fantastic reporter, and there is plenty of evidence to back up his assertion. Treloar was a member of the *Detroit Free Press* team that won a Pulitzer Prize for its reporting on Detroit's 1967 riots. He joined the *Detroit News* in 1969, earning a second Pulitzer nomination while he was there for a series of ecology stories. Treloar's claims to fame also include writing a provocative story about hallucinogens that is credited even today with coining the term "yooper" for someone who lives in the Upper Peninsula. On his untimely death of a heart attack at age forty-seven in 1980, Treloar was quoted as saying, "God deliver me from politicians, government, that weighty stuff. All I want is a good man-bites-dog story."

Tim says his father wrote multiple articles on Louis Tourtois, and the family ate at Loui's pizzeria, as well. His father enjoyed pizza generally and was known for bringing a pie into the newsroom to share from time to time, Tim says.

"He worked for the Sunday magazine back then," Tim says. "He loved doing [the contest]. It wasn't just him; he got lots of reporters involved. He brought the pizzas up to the fourth floor, and there were a ton of them up there, eating pizza. People voted on it.

"I remember him talking about it at home," Tim recalls. "We had big discussions on it. He wrote about Giordano's in the article because we always went there. It was a little strip mall pizza place in Lincoln Park on Fourth Street. We liked it the best when we were kids, so it's what we grew up on."

Business at Giordano's "doubled or tripled" because of Treloar's mention of it in the *Detroit News* pizza contest article. Tim recalls going to school with the Giordano family—"her kids went to the same junior high as us"—and Mrs. Giordano calling their home to thank them for including the pizzeria's name in the famous story.

Here's where the story gets interesting.

"She told us, 'You can have all the free pizza you want. Just let us know,'" Tim says.

Tim says his father refused, being the ethical journalist that he was. However, that message didn't filter down to the whole family.

"Six years later, Mrs. G calls again. 'There's no free pizza for you until you mention us again,'" Tim recalls.

That's when the family found out that one of them had been ordering pizzas from Giordano's regularly based on the article and Mrs. G's offer. No one in the family knew about it because the perpetrator had kept it a secret.

"My dad was stunned," Tim says.

THE *DETROIT NEWS* CONTEST came at a pivotal time in Detroit pizza history for other reasons, as well. As it turns out, the 1970s served as a pinnacle for pizza in terms of who was making it, the style they selected and what was soon to come.

Little Caesars scored fourth in the *Detroit News* pizza contest back in 1970. But by this point, Mike and Marian Ilitch's pizza company had more than fifty locations and was expanding quickly. Mike and Marian Bayoff met on a blind date arranged by his father in 1954. Marian knew food, having grown up in her father's restaurant; she was working as a Delta Airlines clerk when she met Mike. Within months, they were married. Mike was playing baseball for the Detroit Tigers' minor league system but was injured and had to retire in 1955. Around this time, they started thinking about opening a business of their own. On May 8, 1959, the couple opened their first pizzeria, called Little Caesar's Pizza Treat, on Cherry Hill Road in Garden City, a Detroit suburb. The store's name came from Marian's nickname for Mike; according to lore, Mike wanted to call it Pizza Treat. As the story goes, they sold forty-nine pizzas on the first day they opened. In those early years, Marian kept the store's records in a spiral notebook, according to company history. As a largely carryout model, they could keep costs low and grew rapidly.

Three years later, Little Caesars was selling hundreds of pizzas a week but saw an opportunity to boost volume if they concentrated on a lower-priced pizza. As a result, they opened their first franchise in Warren. They started using a Roman-style figure in a toga as their logo, creating a brand icon. Mike and Marian opened their first Detroit location in 1967. By 1969, the company had expanded into Canada and celebrated its fiftieth restaurant. Ten years later, it shook up the industry by selling two pizzas for the price of one, coining the phrase "Pizza!Pizza!" to represent its new offer. By 1987, it had stores in all fifty states.

Other pizza makers like Tony Sacco of Mootz Pizzeria in Detroit and John Jetts of Jet's Pizza say they learned about how to advertise their pies and how to expand a brand from watching what the Ilitch family did. "I learned marketing from Mike Ilitch," Sacco says. "I learned that making a good pizza was secondary to marketing. They kinda hurt the pizza business, because now people weren't making the best pizza. They were trying to make the most affordable pizza."

To grab its share of the Detroit square pizza market, in 1988, Little Caesars introduced its own deep-dish version known as the Pan!Pan. That same year, the company started a national advertising campaign, a sign of just how large the brand had become. By 2020, Little Caesars was the third-largest pizza chain in the United States. In 2022, the chain started using the term "Detroit Style pizza" in its ads, noting the popularity of this pie.

DOMINO'S PIZZA STANDS OUT among pizzerias as the nation's largest chain. Its story begins in 1960 when brothers Tom and James Monaghan opened their first pizzeria, called DomiNick's. The duo had purchased the pizzeria from Dominick DiVarti in Ypsilanti. At first, Tom and James promised to share the work equally, but James soon found the schedule troublesome. James had a full-time job as a mailman, and within eight months, he agreed to trade his half of the business to Tom for the Volkswagen Beetle the pizzeria used for deliveries.

By 1965, Tom Monaghan renamed the business Domino's and added two more locations. A company employee came up with the name, and the company brought that into its logo of a domino with three dots on it to represent its three stores.

"My aim was to make the best possible pizza, so I used the best ingredients I could buy and piled them on," Monaghan said in his 1986 autobiography, *Paper Tiger*, which he co-wrote with Robert Anderson. "But I felt the competition had better sauce than we did, and I didn't know what to do about that. Jerry Garber, a salesman for our supplier, Paul Fata & Sons, told me about an old Italian place in Lansing that had the best pizza sauce he'd ever tasted. I paid the place a visit, and sure enough, I liked its sauce much better than the DiVarti creation we'd been using. To my surprise, the owner didn't hesitate to give me the recipe, and it was a big hit with our customers."

In *Paper Tiger*, Monaghan writes about his research trips, where he visited other pizzerias to gain knowledge and, in some cases, information he could use at his pizzerias.

"Perhaps the most important thing I learned on these research trips was that everyone is convinced that his pizza is the best in town. It didn't matter what kind he was making—thin or deep-dish—and it didn't matter how appealing or awful his pizza was. He thought it was great," Monaghan writes.

"One terrific idea I picked up in our Monday travels came from a place called Dino's in Detroit. It was a well-run operation that later grew into a chain of about 170 stores. I introduced myself to one of the owners, Benny Laquinta, and he gave me a tour of his place. Everything looked familiar enough until I saw them sliding pizzas into the ovens on round screens. That stopped me in my tracks. Benny explained that the screens allowed the heat to get to the pizzas fast enough, and made the pies easier to handle, both going into and coming out of the oven. To put an uncooked pizza in the oven, a pizza maker used to set the pie directly on a wooden paddle or 'peel' that looked like a short-handled oar."

By 1965, Monaghan knew Domino's growth needed to go faster and in more directions. Monaghan created Domino's famous "thirty minutes or less" delivery promise in 1973, and this offering helped boost the brand's sales and reputation within the industry. By 1978, Domino's had 200 pizzerias. Twenty years later, it had 5,000 locations. As of 2020, it had more than 14,400 locations in more than eighty-five countries. According to the company, Domino's delivers more than 1 million pizzas each day all over the world. Monaghan retired in 1988, selling his 93 percent of the business to Bain Capital for an estimated $1 billion.

HUNGRY HOWIE'S WAS THE brainchild of Jim Hearn, a Dearborn native and U.S. Army veteran who, in 1973, took a small Taylor hamburger shop and turned it into a carryout and delivery pizzeria. According to some, Hearn received the nickname "Howie" because employees thought he bore a resemblance to business magnate Howard Hughes. Hearn hired a delivery driver, Steve Jackson, who soon grew into Hearn's business partner. By 1983, the two had awarded their first Hungry Howie's franchise. Three years later, there were more than sixty-five franchises across the state.

According to company lore, Hearn grew weary of Michigan's gray and cold winters. So, he took his part of the business to Florida, and Jackson took over the Michigan portion. Hearn grew his portion of the business to more than two hundred Florida locations, delivering pizzas himself when the mood hit in his Chevy Astro. The chain truly gained fame when it developed and tested flavored crust pizza regionally in 1983 and rolled it out nationally in 1985. By 2020, Hungry Howie's had nearly six hundred stores in twenty states.

At least one person has said the extreme success and popularity of these low-cost, round pies are the reason "Detroit Style pizza" should really be defined as a round pizza. That's a topic for another book, so let's move on.

PART II
....
THE SECOND WAVE

Chapter 8

JET'S PIZZA

*E*ugene Jetts was only in his early twenties, but he already felt like his life had stalled out. On the one hand, he had a good job, working for family at a local supermarket. On the other hand, Eugene knew that if he let other people make his decisions, he'd never become the man he wanted to be.

He wasn't cut out for the grocery business, stocking shelves and walking the store floor day after day. Looking around, Eugene saw there was another way—his cousin had the dream job of running a pizzeria. In the pizza shop, his cousin had everything. He hired people from the community. He was in charge of his own destiny.

So, when that same cousin said he would help Eugene start a pizzeria, that felt like the next right step.

Things started rolling quickly, and Eugene saw his life laid out in front of him. He'd work with his hands. He'd use everything he learned on the job, only he'd be doing it for himself. He'd make his father and mother proud.

Then, he got the phone call that changed his life—only it wasn't the one Eugene expected. Ultimately, it was the worst news Eugene could imagine. His cousin had changed his mind. The deal was over. The conversation and his vision of an independent life ended at the same time. To Eugene, it was more than a business deal gone bad. It was one more hope dashed.

Eugene got into his car and started to drive, his frustration mounting. His parents had told him to get out and get started in the world. Eugene had every intention of doing that.

But how could he get started when the only thing he truly wanted to do had just ended?

Eugene Jetts was born on September 20, 1954, to Eugene and Elmina Jetts. His father, a U.S. Navy veteran who had served in World War II, worked at the Chrysler stamping plant at 15 Mile and Van Dyke, while his mom worked at Ford Motor Company at its trim plant at 23 Mile and Mound. They had three kids: Maryetta, Eugene and John. Elmina was a great cook, and the family ate well at her table.

Around age twenty-two, Eugene was working for his uncle, James Galloway Sr., at Chatham's Supermarket. Uncle Jim wanted Eugene to join him in management, and Eugene was willing to give it shot, his brother, John Jetts, recalls. But those long grocery store hours and the midnight shift proved exhausting, and Eugene left. He had a short stint at Chrysler, and he loved driving the cars off the line. But Eugene would be working for someone else, and his heart, mind and spirit still felt uneasy.

John Jetts was born four years after his brother. His early childhood was mostly following Eugene around, John recalls. John's first job was at his cousin's pizzeria and party store at age fourteen. He mostly picked up hours on the weekends, eventually getting the pizza make line so organized that his cousin had him training guys ten or fifteen years older than him on how to work it.

"I worked there for about three years and just loved making the pizzas, interacting with all of the customers," John says. "A big part, too, was working and training the employees that he was bringing in. Here I am, a kid, and he's telling me to train these older guys. It was a whole different ballgame."

All the while, John says he saw how his brother felt drawn to entrepreneurship.

"I'll never forget the day I was walking through the kitchen. My brother was sitting at the dining room table and he's like, 'Hey, tell me what you're going to do when you're out of school,'" John says. "Eugene said, 'What do you think about opening our own store?'"

Soon enough, Eugene made a deal with his cousin to open another pizzeria, picking out a location in Sterling Heights.

"We were in the process of the build-out and my brother called [our cousin] and said, 'Hey, we're getting closer,' and he's like, 'You know, Gene, I've changed my mind. Do your own gig. I don't want to do it with you guys.' Fine. There we go. Now, it's in our hands," John says.

John was seventeen years old and a high school senior. He wasn't sure what he wanted to do for a living, as he was still just a kid. John says his mom hoped he might go to college and, eventually, become a doctor. But John hated needles, so he knew that wasn't going to happen, he admits.

Brothers Eugene and John Jetts worked together from day one at the pizzeria and party store in Sterling Heights. *Jet's Pizza.*

It became clear that this unexpected dismissal was weighing on Eugene, John says. According to Jet's Pizza lore, Eugene was driving around in Sterling Heights looking for a house to buy when he saw that party store up for lease. Interestingly, it had a pizza oven already installed in the back. Eugene took the only money he had—which was about $20,000 in savings he had set aside for a down payment—and signed the lease papers.

John recalls the story with a laugh. "He's very young. No background in restaurants. And he's got to convince our landlord to give him a lease, and he did it," John says. "We still appreciate [our landlord]; his name is Dave Adams, and he gave us a start. Because a lot of people wouldn't give Eugene a start. But Dave listened to Eugene, loved it and signed the lease."

Throughout his senior year at Sterling Heights Stevenson, John said, his brother worked on getting their store ready to open. Their parents gave Eugene a little money to help, but otherwise, the whole process was on Eugene, he recalls.

John says what he remembers most about that first store was how small it was. It was only 1,200 square feet with about half of that devoted to beer and wine. The other half was for the store's food offerings, which included broiled chicken, mostaccioli, fish dinners and lasagna, made using their mother's recipe. It was the ultimate pizza-party store, John says.

The original Jetts Party Shoppe and Pizzeria in Sterling Heights sold a variety of meals as well as pizza to its customers. *Jet's Pizza.*

John graduated from high school in June, and the opening date for the newly minted Jetts Party Shoppe and Pizzeria was August 26, which meant a short summer for the teen. John says he got to sneak in a couple months of fun before his brother put him to work. They used their mom's recipes and sold two pizzas for the price of one, emulating the deals Little Caesars was offering at the time.

John says Eugene devoted himself to the business and wanted to work all the time. At eighteen, John admits, he wasn't yet that mature. As a result, it was like having a second dad—but this one was even harder on him than the first one.

"I don't regret anything. I always tell people: you do everything when you're young. And we did it," John says. "I'm not going to lie—it was hard working with my brother, day in and day out. And I'm talking 8:00 a.m. to at times midnight or 2:00 in the morning. Imagine that there's just two of us. It's a battle of hours."

There was the business side of it, and then there were fun times, John says. He remembers how he and his brother would sit on milk crates after work or on the cots that they kept in the store, dreaming about what opening additional pizzerias might look like. They imagined the business growing to twenty or thirty stores—but that seemed like a huge dream at the time, John says. The two paid themselves their first paycheck of thirty-five dollars each about seven months after the store opened.

Business picked up quickly. "We had a rocket, dynamite store," John says. In 1981, Eugene told *Crain's Detroit* that they had started to notice longer lines of people coming in for their square pizzas—something that was "then a novelty in Southeast Michigan" and the main offering of distant competitors like Buddy's.

"I noticed that people were coming from farther and farther away to get our pizza," Eugene told reporter Nathan Skid. "People who lived in Livonia but worked in Sterling Heights were driving back here to get it."

Soon enough, the party store became a distraction to the more successful pizza side of the business, Eugene told Biz Spotlight.

"We were selling so much of it that I had to get rid of the party store to make room for a bigger kitchen to make the pizzas. That's literally how it started. From that point on, we just kept expanding," Eugene told the news site. "Back in 1978, 1979, if you really wanted a good pizza, you needed to go to a restaurant and then you paid triple to what you would have paid any carry-out pizzeria. Our whole theory was let's take this restaurant taste and bring it at a carry-out price. Everybody said we couldn't do it but we did do it and that's what made us so successful."

EUGENE AND JOHN OPENED their second store at 15 Mile Road and Schoenherr in Sterling Heights. The manager they were supposed to have fell through, so they split up and John moved to this location. "It was hard, working every day with your brother and now you're working on your own at a young age," John says. That location served only pizza, salads, sub sandwiches and bread. The new focus became learning how to run this new system—the idea was to grow these two fledgling locations into a chain someday.

Those first menus focused on advertising the deep-dish pizza, John said. They weren't imitating the kind of pizza found at Buddy's or Cloverleaf. Rather, the brothers were thinking about the kind of success happening at Little Caesars, John recalls, interested in how to build that kind of store volume.

The brothers also focused on speed, being one of the first carryout pizzerias in Metro Detroit to use a conveyor oven. That took the company to the next level, John said, going from a twenty- to twenty-five-minute cook down to twelve or thirteen minutes. That meant pizzas could be ready for customers in fifteen minutes if they were picking up or thirty-five

The Jetts family dropped the extra *t* in their business name when they started to grow the business. *Jet's Pizza.*

minutes for delivery, putting their place on par with Domino's and other quick-delivery operators.

By the mid-1980s, people had started to ask the brothers how they could get into the business with them, seeing how lines of people were waiting outside the store for the pizza. One sticking point became the company name.

"When we sat down with the lawyers doing our franchise circular, they said, 'You shouldn't go down there with your full last name. Just taking the one *t* off will help it.' And we agreed to that. It was hard seeing that [original] sign go down and the new one go up. But that's the way it had to be," John says.

The Jetts brothers opened their third store at 16 Mile and Dequindre. Things got interesting in 1988 with the fourth location at 13 Mile and Hayes, where they brought their cousins, Jeff and Jim Galloway Jr., into the business.

Jim was fifteen years old when he started working for his cousins. "Eugene always had that vision," Jim says. "I can remember sitting on milk crates drinking Michelob Lights at 14 and Ryan when we got off work. 'We're going to grow this company. We're going to take it public.' He used to throw these crazy things out there. I was fired up."

Soon, Jim and Jeff were working two jobs, and the pizzeria was making good money. Jim was working in finance and accounting for a major automotive manufacturer. Jeff was working construction.

"I'd take my suit off and put pizza clothes on," Jim remembers. "The next day, we'd get up at 6:00 a.m. to do our other jobs and then pizza at night. We were still living at home. We thought we were rich."

But that wasn't enough. "The store started going sideways. We weren't putting 100 percent effort in there. We needed to give our full attention to it," Jim says. "Eugene used to say to the franchisees, 'You gotta get in there and work it.' We still stress that. It comes down from his voice: You have to work the store. You gotta be the owner operator."

Eugene decided: It was time for his cousins to go all in.

"At every meeting, we had to have a Michelob Light because that was Eugene's favorite," John said. "We said, 'One of you are going to have to quit your job.' It was Jimmy that picked to quit. Now he's going to have to sit with his mom and his dad and explain this to him. I think we had an extra beer that night. Eugene said, 'Jimmy, good luck tomorrow. You're going to do good, telling your mom.' We always knew that wooden spoon was going to hit you."

The pain was real: Jim's parents had put him through college, and quitting a good corporate job felt like a mistake. But Jim also knew that the situation was untenable. For example, there were times when he had to review a store plan for Jet's while he was at his day job. John would show up at his office with the plan and some McDonald's fast food as a coverup, saying he was there for lunch.

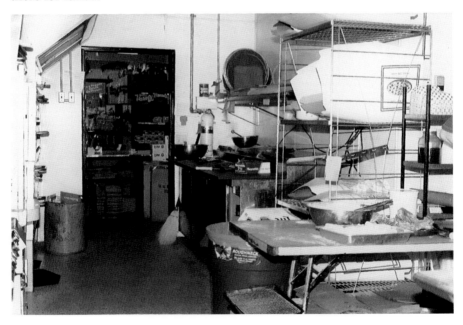

Jet's Pizza grew from a single location to more than four hundred locations around the country, all selling its signature pizza. *Jet's Pizza.*

85

Jim quit, going "full boat," as he says. Besides the family blowback, there were other sacrifices—and some were more difficult than others. For Jeff, that meant his dreams of a little red Corvette.

"I remember Eugene saying, 'Instead of buying the Corvette, why don't you buy the new pizza oven for store four?'" Jeff remembers. "I said, 'No way.' I had the car ordered. John said, 'You can get it later on,' so I had to cancel my order."

Jim remembers it as well. "I remember Eugene saying, 'Put your girlfriend on the oven and you can push her down 13 and Hayes.' I died laughing when he said that."

There were other challenges along the way, including family and relationships. John says girlfriends were often the first to leave.

"The girls that we thought we were going to marry? That didn't happen. Why? Definitely we dedicated ourselves to the business to grow. They either wanted to stay by our side or not. Because with those hours, those fun weekends weren't going to happen," John says.

"They dumped us. We all got dumped," Jim says. "I can laugh about it now. But it wasn't fun back then."

Jeff continued to work in construction until he and Jim opened store no. 6. That was the turning point for Jet's in one way, as the four men formed a partnership to establish Jet's America.

"Jeff and I were fortunate to get involved with both of them in the early days," Jim says. "Eugene had it in him. I always say you either have it or you don't, but Eugene and John had it. They both had a vision of what they wanted to do."

FRANCHISE GROWTH IN THOSE first years was all by word of mouth. John says they started by selling franchises to friends and family. The four owners did the training in person, staying for weeks and attending grand opening celebrations. Making sure they got these openings right was key to the chain's early success, John says. That's because it wasn't just Jet's against the single-store operators. They were competing with Domino's and Little Caesars.

"It took us a while for that to click in our heads," Jim says. "We didn't know anything. I mean, Eugene and Johnny were selling franchises covered in flour out of the back of the 14 and Ryan store."

It wasn't unusual to hold meetings whenever and wherever, John says.

"Back then, we were meeting in alleys with some of these potential franchisees, having a beer, talking to them about what they wanted to do,"

John says. "We'd get off work in pizza clothes and meet in that room with potential franchisees. But we never had maps or thought, 'OK, maybe we should open here first.' It was like, 'I want to open here. I want to open there.' And we just said, 'OK. Go do it.'…Later, we started becoming more calculated and positioning the stores correctly so we weren't taking ourselves out of a two-store market and making it a one-store because we put in a wrong position."

When the growth finally came, it came fast. In 2005, Jet's Pizza opened its one hundredth location. Less than ten years later, it had three hundred franchises up and running across eighteen states.

"We maintain the quality that Eugene and Johnny put together from the beginning when we were kids in that 14 and Ryan store. It has not changed," Jim says.

Chapter 9

VIA 313

*M*ichigan winters can feel endless, as if the gray skies and frigid temperatures are all you'll ever know. Brandon Hunt felt isolated in that darkness, a man without direction. Part of it was the state's long economic malaise. Metro Detroit in 2010 was still recovering from the nation's recession. The resulting slowdown and the state's automotive bankruptcies made it feel like all of Michigan was on pause.

Bearded, tattooed and perpetually dressed in black T-shirts, Brandon saw himself in that same stagnation. The high school dropout wanted to own his own business, but he was perpetually out of work, having been fired yet again. Add in a girlfriend who wanted to talk marriage, and Brandon knew something needed to change.

It started with a phone call to the one person he knew had upended his life and made that transition work: his brother. Zane had the same turbulent childhood, the result of their parents' divorce. Yet Zane finished college, got a good job and now had a wife and children. Even with his new responsibilities, Zane always took Brandon's calls at any hour. Inevitably, the topic always shifted back to their dreams of starting a pizzeria, just like the ones they ate at as kids.

So far, those late-night brotherly confessions had created one tangible thing—a strong draft of a business plan and some proto pizza recipes. In their talks, they agreed that they wanted to open a sit-down restaurant that served their favorite pies, maybe like the ones at Frank's downriver or

Buddy's. But there was a big gap between getting that business plan out of a drawer and getting it out into the world.

"We knew what we wanted, but we didn't know how to get there," Brandon says. "To make that leap? That was the biggest thing."

ZANE HUNT WAS BORN in 1976; his brother, Brandon, came along five years later. Their parents divorced when Zane was ten and Brandon was five. It was a classic romantic mismatch—their parents had married young, and the marriage dissolved. They grew up with their mom, Marlene, in Riverview, south of Detroit. Their mom worked in baggage claims for Republic Airlines, and most weekends, the boys stayed with friends. Sometimes, Zane recalls, they cooked for themselves at home, playing around with a store-bought pizza kit, like those Chef Boyardee ones.

"They'd have this dough mix that came in a little packet. It was really good—it just needed to be doctored up a little bit," Zane says. "Sometimes, it turned out OK, and sometimes, it didn't."

Their mom raised them as best she could, but cooking wasn't exactly her strong suit, the brothers recall. They remember eating out at least three or four times a week, typically pizza or fast food. Zane remembers it as a golden time—what kid doesn't love eating pizza given the chance? They ate it all: Vito's, Clemente's, Trovano's in Southgate. These were the old-time joints, slinging sheet-pan-style pizza inside dining rooms decorated in the colors of the Italian flag—everything was red, white and green. At the time, there were no big players downriver in the pizza scene, Brandon says. Besides the family-owned joints, there was only Little Caesars with its Pizza!Pizza! round pies with standard toppings.

By the time the two brothers were teens, they were working places like Bruno Capella's Riverview's Pizza Place or Angie's. Zane remembers being hired as a delivery driver only to be tasked with every other job in the place: prep, shred cheese, make sauce, make the dough. "It was just good, honest pizza," he says. Brandon got a gig passing out flyers for Capella when he was twelve. Later, Brandon said he did get his own job in a pizzeria, working for Cici's Pizza in Redford for six months, but he ended up getting fired.

Around 1991, Zane says, he remembers seeing his first ad for Buddy's Pizza in the local alt weekly, the *Metro Times*, and wondering what square pizza was all about. They drove into Dearborn to the closest location to try it. Sitting down to eat pizza with servers was an experience. That first trip turned into a regular occasion.

"We knew it was special. We fell in love with Buddy's immediately," Zane says.

After high school, Zane got a degree from a media arts college in Southfield and began working in radio. He got married and started having kids right away. The couple moved to Grand Rapids in 1999, where Zane found work as a morning show producer. Realizing he wasn't making enough money to even buy an entry-level house, Zane pivoted when the couple moved back to Metro Detroit to be near family and his wife's job. After taking a few classes at Grand Valley State University, he used his work experience in information technology to find a job in IT, where he stayed for more than a decade.

Zane remembers how every business trip took him from one town to another, where the minute he was done with the job, he was out on the town cruising for the nearest pizza place. He kept notes of what worked and what didn't. Finding that perfect pie always eluded him, but he knew what he dreamed of making if he ever got a chance to do it for himself.

At this same time, Brandon describes himself as "lost at sea," gravitating to bars for the majority of his working life, moving every time he got into it with a manager or boss and finding a new gig. "You could name a restaurant and I probably worked at it," he says. At twenty-six, he finally got a gig as a general manager at Lions & Tigers & Beers in Wyandotte and moved out of mom's house, feeling like an adult for the first time in his life.

Zane and his family started to think about moving, and Austin felt like the land of plenty: jobs, affordable homes, optimistic people. The only thing the

The Hunt brothers credit their mother, who didn't love to cook, with giving them their love of pizza from an early age. *Hunt brothers.*

city didn't have was a strong pizza scene, Zane says. The pies were good, but Austin felt limited in terms of styles. By this time, Brandon and Zane had an actual business plan, pieced together over months of telephone calls, emails to other pizza makers and lots of meals in other peoples' pizzerias, where the brothers debated how to do pizza their way.

For Zane, it was the right time to leave—until it wasn't. Their mom's breast cancer came back. Only this time, it had metastasized into her brain.

"We found out about it a couple of months before we were scheduled to move to Austin. Those were some hard conversations," Zane says. "I didn't want to leave. But she told me, 'I don't have a future. You do.' I struggled with it. I used to take her to her cancer treatments just north of Chicago in Kenosha. Those drives were us spending real time together."

As their mother's cancer advanced, Zane traveled regularly to Detroit to see her. In one conversation, Zane says, he asked her what she was thinking about at that moment, and she told him: "The unfinished business in my life."

"It felt like she was talking directly to me," Zane says. "I knew from that conversation: we have to do something for ourselves before our time runs out."

ZANE AND BRANDON'S MOTHER died in January 2010. Up to this point, the brothers had been using email to communicate, formulating a recipe for the square pizza they wanted to create. They baked at home a few times a week, logging their ideas in a Microsoft Word document that they shared back and forth.

They also used the fledging tool to meet other pizza makers though a "twenty questions" kind of format. One of the first to respond to their emails was a Detroit pizza guy named Shawn Randazzo, who worked at Cloverleaf; they instantly hit it off. The Hunt brothers also had a pizza blog where they wrote about taste testing other pizzerias, trying to get some knowledge about the industry but also what they liked and didn't like.

But it was all on paper; nothing was real. Things started to ramp up when Brandon finally made the decision to move to Austin. "I'll always remember him calling me on New Year's Eve," Brandon told *Austin Monthly*. "Zane said: 'Why don't we just do something? Come down here and start working on pizza with me.' It was 65 degrees and sunny in Austin, and I was just getting pummeled with snow in Detroit. I just said, 'Man, this is it.'"

The Hunt brothers admit they were infamous for meeting with people to get advice, hoping for an investor or just someone to kick them in the ass and get them moving. Months, then years, passed. Trying to figure out how to build their own Detroit Style pizza business was nearly impossible at the time. One of their longtime mentors, a pizza guy named Dave Ostrander, told them the next step to getting their business up and running. Big Dave said it plainly: They needed to go see the messiah of pizza, the maestro of pie, Tony Gemignani.

Gemignani at the time was a World Pizza Champion, had multiple restaurants and was a two-time Food Network gold medalist. But his biggest claim to fame happened in 2007 when, as a young pizzaiolo, Gemignani went to Italy to compete in a Neapolitan-style pizza contest against the best of the best and won. That feat of creating the Best STG Neapolitan Pizza Margherita—the pizza that made history for putting the food on the world's map—had not only given Gemignani worldwide bragging rights but also lifted him into pizza legend status. Gemignani used that win to open the International School of Pizza in San Francisco, where people of all ages and social stations went to learn from the master.

Zane and Brandon had met Gemignani once at a Pizza Expo, an extravaganza of pizza makers, vendors and wannabes set in Las Vegas. The Hunt brothers fell squarely into the latter category, but that didn't stop them. They printed up some business cards and worked the expo. Gemignani, already a celebrity in the pizza industry, was a keynote speaker. The Hunt brothers chatted him up and exchanged business cards—Gemignani's were real—and agreed to stay in touch.

"We used the fake concept name on the biz cards of Red Top Pies. We didn't like the name at all. We just didn't want to go there empty handed," Zane says.

BACK IN AUSTIN, BRANDON says, the brothers questioned Big Dave. They wanted to do Detroit Style; Tony was known for Neapolitan. Big Dave was adamant: That doesn't matter. Get in with Gemignani. Go do his class. Convinced, the brothers booked a class with Gemignani, bought two tickets to San Francisco with what nickels they could scrape together and arrived at his School of Pizza in October 2010 with the hope that the pizza guru might be the answer to their doubts and questions.

The class itself was small, less than a dozen people, Zane said. The students had Gemignani's complete attention throughout the process, aided by another newbie pizza chef named Jeff Smokevitch. Smokevitch was there as an assistant; he earned his spot from taking a previous class and coming in as the top student. In this new group, some students wanted to go into pizza

The Hunt brothers took a pizza class with Tony Gemignani and Jeff Smokevitch that led them to open a pizza trailer when they got home to Austin. *Hunt brothers*.

as a business; others were home chefs who wanted to level up. They made dough. They studied sauce. Gemignani gave them his recipe for making a world-class Neapolitan pizza and advised the students to tweak it as they saw fit, Brandon says.

"It's just about networking. [Gemignani] probably is the best person you can network with," Zane says. "At the end of Tony's class, he goes around, person by person, in front of the group, and asks you what you're going to do with what you're learning. He gets to Brandon and me, and he says, 'I already know what you guys are going to do. You don't have to make up some marketing campaign. You guys just need to be yourself. That's the best thing you could do. You're two brothers from Detroit who love your city and have lots of pride. Stay on that path.' It was an amazing thing to hear."

In the comfort of that space and atmosphere, chefs traded recipes, insights and promises to keep in touch. Although the mood was congenial, one thing was clear: everyone who knew pizza in that room saw the potential in Detroit Style right away.

"The clock was ticking," Zane says. "We had to be the first to get to market."

THE BROTHERS BEGAN REVISITING their business plan with renewed vigor in early 2011. They had the blessing of the pizza king. All they needed was the money. They started looking for funding in Texas, but without many industry contacts, there wasn't much interest. When they asked around for help in Detroit, the brothers said they were met with a "mafia-esque" silence.

They decided to go it alone. Zane and Brandon put in $20,000 together—everything they had from their mother's life insurance policy. Zane's father-in-law gave another $10,000. They made one crucial shift in their plan. Rather than investing hundreds of thousands of dollars into a sit-down restaurant, they'd start smaller.

Brandon and Zane went on Craigslist and found a food truck that needed a complete gut job. They bought it for likely too much, but that commitment got them moving. Zane and Brandon both were still working their regular jobs, so they renovated the trailer in their off hours. Friends helped. Friends of friends joined in. Guys like Dan Nelson became guardian angels of sorts, making the impossible possible. Nelson helped the brothers find an oven, calling around until he sourced one in San Antonio that not only fit their limited budget but actually fit the truck.

The business account Zane and Brandon had opened together was largely drained by now. But they upped the ante even more, agreeing to a catering gig for one hundred pizzas. That deadline was the push they needed, the brothers say, and they had a functioning pizza truck ready to go on the event day. A small crowd meant they only had to make five pizzas that night, yet it was enough to prove to the Hunt brothers that they had achieved something real. Their first trailer on East Sixth Street felt like a personal victory—they had gone from dreaming about opening a pizzeria to making it happen.

Naming their business now took priority.

"We didn't know if we should play up the Detroit thing—whether we should shy away from it or brag about it. Sometimes people have negative thoughts about Detroit. But we decided to play it up," Brandon told the *Detroit Free Press* in March 2013. "Having Detroit in the name intrigues people. It sparks interest right off the bat."

Maybe...but maybe not. Educating the public as well as the local media became part of the work of marketing this new business. An April 2014 review of the brothers' food remarks, "When the Hunts realized their creations were a novelty down here, they slapped the 'Detroit-style' tag on the pizza. The move was a blend of marketing savvy and a way to rep their allegiance for the hometown. So is the name—313 is Detroit's area code."

Zane and Brandon set up their food truck in December 2011 outside Violet Crown Social Club, a newly opened dive bar that felt like Detroit, Brandon says. The brothers figured out they needed to sell $200 in pizza daily to stay open and give Brandon a salary. That first night, they made $218. Then it was $220, $240, $280. Within four months, they had to hire their first employee because they were doing $1,000 a day.

That food class back in San Francisco was a memory now—but Gemignani's perseverance was nothing to ignore.

"Within months of us leaving Tony's class, he's got Detroit Style on his menu," Zane says. "We were envious. We were jealous. We were anxiety filled. But we resolved to be a part of the new guard. We needed to be positive and friendly. But we had wanted to be the first to do it. We were texting Tony, talking to him about the rollout. He said it was going like gangbusters. Well, no shit. That's because it's really good."

Chapter 10

DETROIT STYLE PIZZA COMPANY

*I*t would be understandable if Shawn Randazzo had been the world's biggest pessimist. His mother, Linda, was a single teenage mom when she had him. Later, she was in an abusive relationship that put her and Shawn's younger brother at risk. Shawn struggled with a record after multiple run-ins with police as a teen. Most people who found themselves in such a situation might feel like they were born unlucky.

Yet Shawn always saw the upside. If he had to work odd jobs to help pay for school clothing, he did. If he wanted a pizza, he folded boxes at the local Domino's to earn one. And when his new boss at the Cloverleaf pizzeria franchise announced he wanted to sell, Shawn convinced Linda to buy into the business with him so they could run it together. Just the thought of becoming an entrepreneur made Shawn's blue eyes glow, Linda says.

What made Shawn different was his motivation, Linda says. It wasn't only about winning; sure, that was nice. It was about showing people who he really was and including them in his wins. He had experienced life's lumps. But that was the past. Since buying the Cloverleaf franchise, getting married and starting to focus on being a father, Shawn had become a self-improvement junkie, taking classes, reading business books and seeking mentors. He studied and worked because he wanted to prove himself, especially when it came to pizza. If he could show people how even a troubled kid like him could grow up to own his own business, he would feel like he had done something special.

Shawn started going to pizza events, gaining a sense of community in his new role. He tested his pizza skills by entering several small contests, winning along the way. In 2012, Shawn had his eyes on the biggest prize yet: World Pizza Champion. It was the industry's most prestigious award. Shawn prepared for months, testing ingredients, baking dozens of batches and making his wife, Keri, and five kids nearly sick of pizza.

His preparation worked: Shawn shocked the Las Vegas crowd of pizza experts and enthusiasts alike by winning the competition. Equally shocking was his pizza, which he proudly described as Detroit Style. People asked for his advice and his autograph like he was some kind of rock star, Linda says. Shawn caught the eye of pizza celebrities as well, including Tony Gemignani.

Back home in St. Clair Shores, Shawn knew life had to change. He likely thought about Tony, who had once worked for his brother and was now operating his own brand. Shawn loved Cloverleaf's owners. Marie and Jack Guerra were like family, and he admired their devotion to Gus Guerra's memory and his pizza. At the same time, Shawn wanted to stand on his own.

But breaking out also meant breaking up one of the most important relationships of his life.

SHAWN PAUL RANDAZZO WAS born on January 24, 1976, in the middle of a storm—foreshadowing his turbulent childhood. His mother, Linda Michaels, was seventeen when she had Shawn; his father left when he found out she was pregnant. Linda describes Shawn as a "community baby," as everyone helped her take care of him while she finished high school.

"He was a really good baby. He was able to be content by himself, and he played well with others. He didn't get into trouble much," Linda says. "But he was a ham and full of energy. He loved being around people. He was very intelligent. At the age of two, he was actually telling stories clearly. And it was funny because I always say I couldn't wait until he could talk, and then I couldn't wait until he shut up."

Linda married and had a second son, Charlie. The family moved several times, living on and off in Detroit and the suburbs. Shawn loved sports, Linda says, playing neighborhood basketball and collecting sports cards. Money was tight, so if Shawn wanted to add to his clothing budget for name brands, he did chores like painting addresses on curbs or offering to take people's garbage out for twenty-five cents a bag, Linda says.

Shawn got his first pizza gig when he was eleven, folding boxes for the nearby Domino's franchise. "They would put us in the back room and give

Shawn Randazzo was an easy baby in that he enjoyed the attention of everyone around him as the first grandchild, his mother, Linda, recalls. *Randazzo family.*

us five bundles of boxes, and we'd sit there for an hour or two folding boxes. Our reward would be a small pizza each at the end of the day. At the time, it was awesome," Shawn told pizza magazine *PMQ.*

His second gig was at the Vineyard, a part store at Mound and Hall Roads. Ironically, the Vineyard sold pizza slices and used Cloverleaf's dough. When he turned eighteen, Shawn saw an opening for a delivery driver at the Cloverleaf carryout franchise on Harper Avenue in St. Clair Shores. The location's owner, Shawn Grafstein, says he remembers hitting it off with Shawn immediately despite the difference in their ages.

"He was hard working and ambitious," Grafstein says. "He became my key guy when he came on board."

Shawn did every job inside the carryout franchise, making himself indispensable. Earning Grafstein's trust, Shawn suggested he help take over some of the long hours. Grafstein, who had four children, agreed, and Shawn began working Sundays. When Grafstein told Shawn he wanted to sell the Cloverleaf franchise, Shawn had mixed feelings, Linda says. He was disappointed to lose a mentor, but he also felt the itch to buy the business. The challenge was finding the funds. Shawn was twenty-one years old and had a record. Linda was thirty-seven, newly divorced and working as a waitress.

"It felt like a second full-time job, looking for bank financing," she recalls. They finally got the money together through a small credit union loan,

Linda's home refinance and a land contract. It was 1997, and they had put everything on the line. Now, they had to figure out how to make it work. Those first months were brutal, Linda recalls. The mother-and-son team felt thrown into the business without a playbook.

"At the beginning, it was just me and him, and we would work sixty to eighty hours a week," Linda says.

SHAWN KNEW THE BUSINESS was stagnating and something had to change. He and Linda felt like they were working nonstop. In 2005, Shawn told the *Smart Pizza Marketing* podcast he needed to get his own version of a business degree, even if he had to fashion it together by himself.

"I made a pact with myself to educate myself. Never stop learning," Shawn said on the podcast. "I didn't have a business background. I only had entrepreneurial spirit. I started taking classes, listening to consults, reading books. I plugged myself into the expos. I went to all of the industry events available. It was like a turning point."

Shawn also felt ready to put his pizza-making skills to the test, and pizza contests seemed like the best way to gain credibility and name recognition.

Linda Michaels was a teenager when she got pregnant with Shawn, and she says their struggle in the early years made them closer as a family, which grew to include brother Charlie (*right*). *Randazzo family.*

Linda says Shawn talked about participating in these contests and pizza expos as a winning strategy. Pizzerias that attended not only learned from one another, but they also got great publicity if they won.

His winning streak started in 2009 when Shawn went to Columbus, Ohio, for the North American Pizza and Ice Cream Show. Shawn attended as a Cloverleaf representative, entering the chain's Meat Supreme pizza into the competition. Shawn won and dedicated the award to his mentor, Cloverleaf founder Gus Guerra.

In his *PMQ* interview, Shawn said he remembered being surprised that Detroit Style wasn't a thing in Ohio.

"I was the only one there out of 60 or 70 competitors, three-and-a-half hours outside of Detroit, that had a square pizza with caramelized cheese and sauce on top. It fueled the passion in me to really put this style of pizza on the map," Shawn said. "Before that, I literally thought this style of pizza was everywhere, but I didn't realize it was such a secret to our region. So, I said, 'We got this amazing culinary masterpiece that came from this region that nobody knows about,' and I thought I could also put some positive light on the city as well."

Linda says Shawn came home with a new goal.

"When he won in Ohio, nobody knew what Detroit Style pizza was. They were laughing, saying it was probably pizza with bullet holes or a copy of Little Caesars," Linda remembers. "And then he won first place. That put a burning fire in his belly. That was his passion now: to get Detroit Style pizza as well known as Chicago or New York."

At the beginning of 2011, Shawn advanced to the finals at the International Pizza Expo in Las Vegas; he eventually won Best Pizza in the Midwest and placed sixth for Best Non-Traditional Pizza. He won again in September 2011 when he entered the American Pizza Championship in Orlando, scoring third place. In a self-published press release, Shawn called Detroit Style pizza "the Motor City Secret" and "the unsung hero of landmark pizzas."

"I'm grateful to serve Gus Guerra's authentic pizza recipe, first introduced more than 60 years ago. I'm proud and passionate about our pizza, and excited to be on the forefront of putting Detroit-style pizza on the map," Shawn said in that same press release.

Right before he left for the 2012 Pizza Expo, Shawn did an interview with *Pizza Today* magazine on behalf of Cloverleaf.

"Our pizza has a deep history, and we are fortunate enough to serve Gus Guerra's recipe that was first introduced in 1946," Shawn wrote. "In the next five years, we plan on opening several more Cloverleaf Pizza Carryout

& Delivery locations. We plan on opening a third location by fall of 2012. Franchising may come to play in 2013. Besides growing our business, I think personal growth comes hand in hand, so we plan on investing in our key employees and ourselves consistently and continuously."

Around the same time, Linda says, the mother-and-son partnership was looking to sign a new contract with Cloverleaf. Linda admits she and Shawn had some concerns about the contract they had with the Guerra family at that time—it was a sparse two pages, and they worried that if Jack Guerra's sons were to take over the business, the two of them could find themselves out of luck. Jack had never shared the recipe for the dough, protecting it for Cloverleaf.

"They could cut us out of it," Linda says. "We wanted to make the contract better and Shawn wanted the recipe for the dough."

AROUND THIS SAME TIME, Linda says she and Shawn started looking for another location. The 2008 recession had hit Metro Detroit hard, and there were some inexpensive storefronts for lease. They found a site at 21 Mile and Hayes roads, even going so far as to sign the paperwork. Shawn updated their website with the new location, excited about its potential and the good deal they had received.

That's when Shawn got a call from Jack Guerra at Cloverleaf. Jack told him they couldn't open a location there because the Guerras were preparing to open one up just a mile away. For Shawn, the time had come; he needed to be on his own.

By the time he arrived in Las Vegas, Shawn had made up his mind. He brought with him the dough recipe he'd developed and planned to use during the competition. If his pizza came in second, third or any other position, Shawn knew he had something good on his hands, Linda says. If his dough lost? Well, he would figure it out from there.

Shawn won. And everything changed.

When Shawn returned home, he issued a press release to announce the next phase in his life. "In mid-summer 2012, Cloverleaf will be transitioned to their new brand, Detroit Style Pizza Co., which will serve Randazzo's new award-winning pizza recipe," the press release said. "Detroit Style Pizza Co. was born out of my passion for the perfect pizza. The new signature recipe is not the same pizza served by Cloverleaf. It tastes even better and passed the ultimate test by winning at the International Pizza Expo."

Shawn Randazzo (*middle*) joined the World Pizza Champions team, which also included Jeff Smokevitch and its founder, Tony Gemignani. *Tony Gemignani.*

Winning in Las Vegas had seemed impossible. Now, anything was possible.

"He really had the personality for it," recalls Jeff "Smoke" Smokevitch, another Michigan native and owner of Denver's Blue Pan Pizza. Smoke competed side by side with Shawn at several Pizza Expos, narrowly losing to Shawn in 2012. "You can't throw somebody passive who can't control their nerves into that setting. You have to be the right person to do these competitions well. Shawn was that person."

SHAWN BECAME THE BIGGEST cheerleader for Detroit Style, steadfastly believing it could be a major player in the pizza industry. "Even when we doubted it, he was promoting Detroit Style like nobody else and like nobody else ever will," Smokevitch says.

Grafstein agrees. "You could see a change in him and a seriousness about getting the Detroit Style pizza out in the world."

On the *Smart Pizza Marketing* podcast, Shawn said that win "lit a fire" in him. "After winning World Pizza Champion maker of the year, I branched off and launched my own company, taking my personal mission and making it my company mission to increase awareness of authentic Detroit Style pizza by sharing its history, teaching people how to do it authentically and creating memories and opportunities for people," he said.

Linda says Shawn also understood that Detroit Style pizza had another revenue stream hidden in plain sight. "Shawn used to say, 'You know who made the money in the California gold rush? The people who sold the picks, shovels and pans,'" Linda says.

Not only did Shawn put up a website where he could offer his expertise as a consultant, but he also created a separate entity to sell the flour, dough mixes and pans that a pop-up, trailer or restaurant might need if they wanted to start selling the style. He started a distribution business from his basement, selling the pans and related equipment needed to make a Detroit Style pizza—even if most of the world was still asking what exactly that was at the time.

Another part of the business expansion was Shawn's training classes. Perhaps this was another nod to his hero, Tony Gemignani. But it was also a marketing move on Shawn's part, creating disciples of his methods and products.

"My whole idea behind it was I can't get the word out myself. It's going to take an army of people to know how to do this the right way," Shawn told *Smart Pizza Marketing*. "When someone says Detroit Style pizza they're saying, 'Oh yeah, Little Caesars.' There's a night and day difference between an authentic version to some of these other big chain versions of Detroit Style pizzas. How to execute, make this style authentically—word will spread a lot faster."

Potential pizza makers were happy to have Shawn's help. They flew into Metro Detroit to meet with him for in-person classes or brought him out to their locations for training. Mike Spurlock was one of those guys trying to come up with his own recipe for Detroit Style, getting close enough that the former Detroiter's friends in his new hometown of Louisville were telling him he should open his own restaurant.

"This was 2012, and there wasn't a lot of good information on the Internet. There was a blog here and there, and there were a couple people getting closer to the recipe. But no one had really cracked the code," Mike says. "I read about Shawn in *Pizza Today* magazine, and I realized then Detroit Style might have some legs. It might just be time for me."

Mike emailed Shawn without an introduction—just a friendly inquiry. Mike says he was surprised when Shawn answered right away. Mike flew to

Metro Detroit and met with Shawn at his St. Clair Shores carryout location. For days, Shawn walked through Mike's business plan, offered suggestions and taught Mike his recipe.

"On the first day, he said, 'I'll make mine. You make yours.' And we worked side by side. We put them in the oven and had them for lunch," Mike says.

Just like many of his students, Mike bought his Detroit Style pans from Shawn. Within a year of that visit, Mike had opened Loui Loui's in Lexington, introducing a new city to Detroit Style pizza and calling Shawn regularly, more for the comradery than anything else, he says.

"Here's this guy out of Detroit, and he starts going to the competitions and *boom*! He starts winning. That's what gave me the confidence to go out and do my thing," Mike says. "He was indominable personality. He had to elbow his way into it."

There are dozens of similar stories. Many pizza company owners credit Shawn for not only teaching them the Detroit Style recipe but also sharing his friendship and advice afterward.

"He put [Detroit Style pizza] on the map," says Trinity, Shawn's daughter. Linda agrees. "Shawn was the only one who wanted Detroit Style pizza to be well known. Everyone else wanted it hush-hush. They felt like if we tell people, we're going to lose business. Shawn was the opposite."

Shawn also became interested in the business potential of frozen pizzas and working with a distributor. Like many other pizzerias, he got started with half-baked pies that he could freeze and sell to people who lived outside of Michigan or wanted to send some pizzas to expats. One customer regularly ordered a dozen pizzas each month, all sent to her home in Florida. Shawn worked with online food distributor Goldbelly to formalize his offerings, and his frozen pizza numbers started to tick up.

Those kinds of pizza fanatics who stock up on their favorite pies were Shawn's favorites, he told *PMQ*, recalling a time when he went out of his way to help someone hungry for Detroit Style.

"Many years ago, I get a call, and it was from this lady saying that her father was in the hospital dying of cancer. One item on his bucket list was to get a good, authentic Detroit Style pizza. They used to live in Detroit but now lived in Texas with no access to it," Shawn said.

"At the time, we did send pizzas with customers that used to winter in Florida, but we didn't really do mail order. But I said, 'Of course!' So, I got the information and sent the package out the next day," Shawn said, recalling how he had to send the pies a couple of times because the first

Shawn Randazzo traveled around the country and, later, the world, to teach others how to make Detroit Style pizza. He went to Louisville to work with Mike Spurlock (*left*) and Michelle Spurlock. *Mike Spurlock.*

package was damaged. "She called back after that and wanted to tell me how much it meant to their family and that her father wanted to talk to me on the phone; was this possible? I said, 'Absolutely!' So, we set the call up for the next day.

"The next day, I get on the phone with this guy, and he just went on and on about how when he was younger, he and his friends would go out and get pizza. He was just reliving all these memories with me. He sounded like a teenager," Shawn recalled. "I was thinking to myself: How could this man be dying of cancer? He sounded so full of life. It was all because of the pizza memories. The memories [of] pizza brought up his youth and good times.

"He ended up passing about a month later, and after that whole experience, I get a really long letter from the family that brought me tears, basically saying that this gift of pizza brought the family together again one more time before he passed. Sharing, talking and making memories," Shawn said. "That's the power of pizza."

Chapter 11

BLUE PAN PIZZA

Giles Flanagin had everything he'd ever wanted by his mid-thirties: a high-flying real estate career, a real estate portfolio worth millions, good friends, a girlfriend he wanted to marry. Years of hard work and sacrifice had made everything come together for the kid who grew up mowing lawns in the Metro Detroit suburbs.

Then came the 2007–08 economic crash, which demolished the real estate market across the country. Giles's business partnership collapsed. He needed a new job and another opportunity—fast.

A single phone call gave him the out he needed. It was his elementary school buddy Jeff Smokevitch. Jeff, known to his friends as Smoke, needed help. Smoke's first pizzeria in Telluride was going well, and the partners wanted to open another location in Denver. Giles had the construction and real estate background Smoke needed.

After long deliberation, Giles and his girlfriend decided Smoke's offer was the best they had. They packed what little they had left and headed west. While driving across the country, Giles realized this was his best and possibly only chance to change his life. Smoke had a location secured for Brown Dog Pizza, and the buildout would be relatively simple.

Once Giles got to Denver, plans quickly changed. A neighborhood association didn't want another sports bar slinging drinks till all hours of the morning. When Giles met with the association, the meeting flopped.

"They said, 'Get ready for the fight of your life,'" Giles recalls. "I tried to explain we were going to be a family-style pizzeria, but there was zero talking.

They didn't want to hear anything. It was the end of the conversation.... They shredded us."

The City of Denver denied their liquor license request, ending any aspiration of opening Brown Dog Pizza in Denver. Once again, Giles found himself at a crossroads.

He decided to take a job working for the City of Denver, giving him plenty of time to think about how his life had gone awry.

"I lost literally everything," Giles says. "I had less money in the bank than I did when I was in college."

THE GRADE SCHOOL FRIEND who called Giles that day was Jeffrey Smokevitch, whose Michigan loyalties run deep. Smoke was born in Birmingham, a wealthy Metro Detroit suburb in affluent Oakland County, and he attended Seaholm High School, where he was known as a hardcore athlete. It was the kind of town where kids set up lemonade stands, and Smoke remembers setting up a hot dog stand with his brother as a kid.

"We made a giant sign out of a two-by-four that went across the whole road, so cars had to stop and buy a hot dog before they could pass," Smoke told *Westword* magazine.

Birmingham is known for its upscale downtown shopping district and equally high-end restaurants, including several beloved local pizzerias. Smoke says his favorite as a kid and even today is Primo's, an Italian mainstay and the first place he visits whenever he comes home. He got his first restaurant job as a teen, working as a dishwasher and busboy.

Smoke attended the University of Michigan, where he was a member of the varsity football team that won two Big Ten Conference titles and the 1997 National Championship. He graduated with a bachelor of arts in economics. A short postgraduation vacation to the Denver area became permanent when he decided skiing was more interesting than finance.

"I went to Telluride on a ski trip for a couple weeks. I'm still here, more than twenty years later," Smoke says.

In Telluride, Smoke worked a series of jobs. He ended up at Pacific Street Pizza, a little carryout joint where he was making about ten dollars an hour, the going rate in 2001. That first season, Smoke says, he remembers being stuck on the grill or fryer despite his repeated requests to learn how to make pizza. After he had been there for about a year, he finally got a chance to throw a few pies, and he was hooked. Around that time, one of the two partners at Pacific Street said they wanted to sell their share of the business,

Jeff Smokevitch went from his hometown of Birmingham to Ann Arbor, where he played for the Michigan Wolverines, and then on to Denver, where he eventually found a job at a pizzeria. *Blue Pan.*

and Smoke was interested. The new ownership changed the name to Brown Dog Pizza.

At Brown Dog, Smoke says, he worked on perfecting his idea of the perfect pie. That pizza combined all his most formative pizza memories from the Metro Detroit area and Birmingham proper. He lived down the street from Primo's, he was a block from a Jet's Pizza and there was a Buddy's less than a mile away from his home.

The bottom of the pie had to be crispy, like Jet's Pizza. The interior crumb came from Primo's. "It's really soft—it might be too dense and doughy for some people," Smoke says. Most importantly, the rest of the pizza Smoke dreamed of had to be like Buddy's, with the cheese around the edges and the caramelization it created for that crispy bite.

"I took things from each one that I liked; that was the flavor profile and texture that I was going for," Smoke says.

He started serving his recipe at Brown Dog, calling it a Sicilian pizza. "One night, a customer asked to talk to me. He was really fired up," Smoke says. "We were yelling at each other, and he told me we weren't making a Sicilian pizza."

Smoke admits he made the customer leave but later checked out a true Sicilian recipe. "I was doing it wrong, and calling it a Sicilian," he says. "I figured I better figure it out or start doing something else."

Smoke says he worked on the recipe over and over, but he couldn't quite get it there—it wasn't the taste he wanted yet. That's when he got the idea to attend one of Tony Gemignani's pizza classes to up his game, imagining making the ideal Detroit square but doing it in his newly adopted hometown.

Did he ever think of going back to Detroit to learn those same lessons? Smoke says back then, no one was willing to make that happen.

"Part of my feeling defeated [by Detroit Style] at that time was how secretive Detroit is about the pizza," Smoke says. "It's the same in New York or Chicago, honestly. It's the time that these chefs grew up in—they're really secretive....I went into [my favorite pizza places] and asked about oven temps and other things, and I got no answers. I learned from Big Dave [Ostrander] that the old way they had to do it was go into dumpsters and find the empty flour bags and other ingredients to find out how they're doing it."

TONY'S CLASS WAS A revelation, Smoke recalls. Gone were the secrets and cold stares he found in Metro Detroit's pizza industry. Instead, he found the pizza savant was an open book.

"Tony swings the gate the other way. He teaches all of the newbies. He tells you, 'Anything you want to know, I'll tell you. I'm not keeping any secrets.' That's how I learned," Smoke says.

Smoke had met Tony casually at the Pizza Expo earlier that year, and he felt certain that the chef would help him unlock the Detroit square recipe. He showed up for that July session ready to learn. Tony's class is grueling in some ways, Smoke says. It is a weeklong intensive for people who want to open pizza restaurants that takes you from early morning into a nighttime restaurant service at one of Tony's restaurants. In between, you're studying and preparing for the final test. If you graduate, you have the kind of training that gets you ready to put up your own shingle and start slinging dough.

At week's end, Tony holds a competition for the class: they have to search San Francisco for the pizza ingredients they want and then put together a pie for tasting. Smoke ended up winning, and as a result, he was invited back to serve as Tony's sous-chef at another class. Smoke says he was down with the additional training, knowing that anything Tony could teach him would be hugely valuable.

"Anybody who knows Jeff very well understands that once Jeff decides to do something, he goes in very hard, whether it's skiing, becoming a vegetarian or making pizza," Giles Flanagin says. "He has that kind of brain. When he makes a conscious decision to do something, he puts the pedal down."

That second class in October 2010 is where Smoke met the Hunt brothers.

"Tony does this thing where he goes around the room and asks everyone, 'Why are you here?' And [Zane] and Brandon say it's because they want to make Detroit Style pizza," Smoke recalls. "I started thinking in my head, 'Holy shit! Someone from Detroit wants to do what I've been thinking about forever.' I had been testing a pizza that had been a total flop, and I felt defeated by my trial and error being so bad. So, when the Hunt brothers said that, it was a great moment."

During the class, Smoke says, they talked about Detroit Style pizza, trying to come up with different doughs and hydrations. Tony listened, as well, remembering what he could from the time he had traveled as a young pizza chef to Detroit and tried a few varieties. The enthusiasm in the room sparked something in Tony, as well, Smoke says, and the energy was electric.

"When we all went home from the class, I kept practicing, testing. We kept calling and emailing one another, developing our dough recipes. That class gave me the courage and inspiration I needed," Smoke says. "We were all comrades in battle. If we were going to fail, we were all going to fail together."

GILES FLANAGIN MET JEFF Smokevitch when the two began attending Pembroke Elementary. Giles grew up in Troy, a Metro Detroit suburb about forty minutes north of Detroit filled with office complexes, shopping centers and McMansions. Giles says he was entrepreneurial at an early age, mowing lawns with a buddy by age twelve. By the time Giles got to high school, he'd become the "long-haired, hippy kid" to Smoke's football star. They stayed friends throughout, even after Smoke ended up at University of Michigan and Giles went to Flagstaff, where he got a degree in finance from Northern Arizona University.

Giles describes his path as a mix of winging it and needing a change of scenery. He graduated in 1999, and his parents gave him an unusual graduation gift: a $300-a-month stipend that would last for six months and no more. Giles ended up getting a studio apartment in Chicago, sleeping on the floor for the first few months until he could afford a bed. Chicago was booming in the early 2000s, and Giles ended up in a real estate career. He worked his way up from faxing documents and completing residential punch lists to becoming a minority partner at a small development firm to cofounding a real estate consulting group with a longtime childhood friend. Things felt like they were on the right track, Giles says.

He and his brother visited Smoke in 2008, eating at Brown Dog. Something inside of Giles said this was the place he needed to move.

"I was sitting at Brown Dog, and I told Smoke: 'If you ever bring this to Denver, please call me first.' I have no experience in restaurants other than being a waiter. But I knew that with our two skill sets, we were complementary. I had a grasp of small business, and Smoke had this passion and drive to make really good pizza," Giles says.

Back in Chicago, Giles says, his business partnership expanded to include a third partner, and that is where everything started to change. By that winter, Giles had been kicked out of the partnership, and he was in debt up to his eyes.

"I was sitting on my back porch, and I got a call from Smoke. He tells me that he and his partner in Telluride [Dan Lynch] have just signed a lease in Denver to start a Brown Dog there. They wanted to know if I would come west and manage the buildout," Giles says. "Smoke knew how tough things were for me, and this was a way for me to own a part of the business and contribute my worth. I told him, 'Yes.'"

Giles packed up and drove to Denver. He was living in a friend's basement, hoping that this pizzeria might be the start of something new and important in his life.

But that vacant space on South Gaylord Street in downtown Denver where Smoke and Giles were building out Brown Dog had riled up the locals, who saw it as a potential sports bar. The South Gaylord Neighborhood Association fought the new pizzeria's application for a liquor license, effectively shutting down the project. At that time, Smoke had spent more than $120,000 of his own money to get the pizzeria off the ground.

"Jeff and his partner had put up all of the money, so they canceled the lease. They went back to Telluride, and I'm in Denver alone. I didn't have any money left," Giles says. "It was awful. I was at a point where if I didn't catch a break soon, I would have to pack up and move back to my parents' house."

In 2012, Giles went with Smoke to the Pizza Expo, where Smoke competed against Metro Detroit's Shawn Randazzo. While Smoke lost by less than a point to Shawn Randazzo's Detroit Style pie, a spark was lit, Giles says.

"That was the first time Detroit Style won at the Expo, and people were asking about it," Giles says. "That was an epiphany for Jeff and me, although we didn't realize it at the time."

In 2013, Smoke won his first world championship in Las Vegas at the International Pizza Competition. By 2014, the duo was ready to try a restaurant again. This time, they kept the investment between the two of them, and they decided to focus the menu on Detroit Style pizza.

"It's amazing what adversity can do; it will make you either focus or fold," Giles told *Westword* magazine. Smoke agrees: "I walk around with a chip on my shoulder for sure—which makes you better."

They started throwing around possible names, and they came up with the idea of calling the place Blue Pan after the steel pans used in Detroit to make the square pizza they both grew up loving.

"I was tasked to do the real estate because Jeff was going back and forth between Telluride and Denver," Giles says. "I would go on Craigslist every day, checking it for listings. I'd call around to brokers. I'd drive the neighborhoods, looking for signs. That's when I found this existing pizzeria that was offering its space for rent."

The space that formerly held Basil Doc's Pizzeria felt right, and the location was great, Giles says. But no one wanted to finance the project. Smoke and Giles did what they had to do—both put up their houses as collateral for the space, and they were able to move in.

"It was scary as shit. You doubled down when your house is collateral and you also have a kid at home....I was still working for the City of Denver full time, and my wife had just given birth to our daughter, and she also worked full time," Giles says. "I was leaving the house at 6:00 a.m. to do paperwork, pay bills and enter invoices. Then I'd go to work until 4:30 p.m., drive back to the shop, put on a T-shirt and get to work. I did that seven days a week for about fourteen months. We had no money to pay me a salary, so I had to work a full-time job outside Blue Pan until things changed for us financially."

The pizza was coming together as well, and Smoke felt like it was the Detroit Style he wanted to serve. But the locals felt otherwise. What made it worse was the derision customers also felt toward the city itself, Giles says.

"People made fun of Detroit, asking if we put motor oil instead of olive oil in our pans. Or they'd ask us if we used bullets," Giles says. "At the time, we also were the most expensive pizzeria in town because no one else was doing high-end or quality ingredients like Smoke wanted to do."

It's an old pizza adage that the first pizza a person tries tends to inform what they think of the dish from that point forward, and that was certainly the case for both people in Denver as well as visitors from Detroit, Giles says. People from all geographic areas simply found it difficult at best and impossible at worst to either accept what Blue Pan was creating as the same thing they had eaten in Detroit or embrace it as a new style.

"When we opened, we were just mocked left and right," Giles says. "Nobody knew what Detroit Style was. Nobody. We had to educate everybody. Even Michiganders who were visiting asked us if we made it up. They'd say there's no such thing as Detroit Style pizza. They only knew it as square pizza. They were saying we made it up or that it doesn't exist."

PART III

THE THIRD WAVE

Chapter 12

THE DELUGE

*A*s a chef, people say Matt Hyland is part genius and part curmudgeon. One of his favorite kitchen mantras goes something like this: "Keep everything sharp, hot and work faster." Matt worked his way up to gain a reputation in the competitive New York food scene for his talent of combining everyday ingredients to create something uniquely craveable.

After years in the kitchen, the chef started to think about opening his own restaurant. Several starts and stops later Matt decided to focus on pizza, a food he was familiar with and loved. But contrarian that he was, Matt also wanted to make something different than trendy Neapolitan.

The best candidate? Detroit Style.

Matt started his research in an untraditional way: he and his then-wife, Emily, ordered, ate and dissected a bunch of frozen Buddy's pizzas to try out. He worked on his own interpretation in the spirit of Detroit and its deliciously doughy base. The couple opened the first Emmy Squared in 2016 with their version of Detroit Style pizza as the star of the menu. Matt's instinct was right on the money: the timing and choice of pizza was ideal.

The Hylands are perfect examples of the Third Wave—pizza makers who expanded what Detroit Style pizza could be in ways that Gus Guerra or those who followed him could never have predicted. Like many who would emulate them, the Hylands did not visit Detroit before opening up their own pizza restaurant that served this style as its signature pie. Matt Hyland never worked in the kitchen with Jimmy Bonacorsi. He wasn't mentored by Louis Tourtois. He never took a class with Shawn Randazzo.

All it took was a bunch of frozen pizzas and an understanding of what this style could be in the right hands.

THE HYLANDS' STORY STARTS in Rhode Island, where the couple met while attending Roger Williams University. They had their first date while still living in the dorms, eating an olive-and-pepperoni pizza. The Jersey girl fell in love with the Brooklyn boy, and they moved to New York together. Matt had studied information science, but now he started working in kitchens. A chance meeting with a recruiter got him to enroll in the Institute for Culinary Education; he graduated in 2004. Emily worked as a teacher and yoga instructor.

Matt grew restless after a decade in the kitchen and wanted to open his own place. He had helped open Sottocasa, a pizza place in their Brooklyn neighborhood, and he knew this was the path he wanted to take. Matt and Emily's first pizza place, Brooklyn Central, failed. Matt says that, looking back, he and his partners had different visions of where they wanted to go in pizza. The couple tried again in 2013, finding a small twenty-six-seat restaurant in Clinton Hill, Brooklyn, that they named Emily. Matt worked in the back making wood-fired artisanal pizza while Emily covered the front

Matt Hyland opened Emmy Squared with his then-wife, Emily, as a tribute to his version of Detroit Style pizza after he realized what an ideal platform the pizza was for his ideas. *Emmy Squared.*

of the house. In fall 2014, *Saveur* magazine ranked Brooklyn as its no. 1 food destination that year, and Emily was the must-try hot spot. The dining room that was supposed to feel like a cozy living room now felt crowded—they needed to grow and find another location.

That led to a second restaurant, this time in the West Village of Manhattan. In that moment, Neapolitan-style pizza was all the rage, but the idea of making the same pizza as everyone else made Matt cringe. The couple heard about Detroit Style, and they looked online to see who was making it. To do their research, they ordered Buddy's Pizza shipped frozen to them at home, trying it over and over until they figured out the basic recipe. Add in a lot of Internet research, and they had a version that felt like their take on the pizza Detroit had been known for since the 1940s.

"We did a lot of Buddy's taste testing and looking at the structure of the pie," Emily says. "We wanted to create our pizza in the spirit of what that was. It was a back door. We didn't set out to make Detroit Style pizza. We wanted *frico* crust with focaccia. So, what's going to get us there?"

"It happened to be that Detroit was the ideal pizza that we had always been looking for, but we didn't know it," Matt says.

Detroit Style was an ideal entry point to establishing an Emmy Squared signature, Matt says, and that goes for many pizza makers who followed the couple's success.

"Even if you use nice ingredients, [Detroit Style pizza] is still relatively inexpensive to make compared to wood-fired pizza because you don't need expensive equipment to get started, like a wood-fired oven. You just need a bunch of pans, which aren't that expensive," Matt says. "It's a much easier entry point. It's easy to learn. It's a pizza that can be made by a less-skilled person who wants to get into it."

It was the pizza they wanted to make based on Matt's expertise and Emily's marketing knowledge. They presented it to New Yorkers, who accepted it as not only delicious but also what "Detroit Style" is.

As a result, Emmy Squared grew from a single location in 2016 to a chain with locations in Nashville, Philadelphia, Louisville, North Carolina, Virginia, Atlanta, California and Washington, D.C. Their fame was as great as their pizzas—by 2017, they had contributed recipes to *People* magazine, and they had been on the best-of lists for everyone from Eater to *Bon Appétit* to Zagat. Peoples' love affair with their pizza continued even as the couple divorced and brought on new business partners to help grow the company. Emily even teaches classes on how to make Detroit Style pizza, and their restaurants have hosted pizzaioli wannabes from around the globe.

Matt says he eventually got to Detroit—but it wasn't until years later. He visited all the kitchens of the major Detroit makers, including Buddy's, Loui's, Cloverleaf and Shawn Randazzo's Detroit Style Pizza Company. The first thing Matt realized, based on his experience in New York, is that Big Apple chefs were using the same dough for their round pies when they made Detroit Style. The result was a dense, thick crust with no aeration. Emmy Squared always used a special recipe designed for Detroit pies, and they put it in the restaurant's pans to let it rise—just like Buddy's and the rest of the OGs did.

The second thing Matt realized? "I was watching what they did, and we do the same thing without knowing what they did," Matt says.

WHAT DIFFERENTIATES THE THIRD Wave from the original Detroit Style pizza makers can be boiled down to a single word: confidence. For these chefs, confidence is the feeling that you can trust not only yourself but also others. You can rely on people to help you or the fact that you know the truth about a situation. Matt Hyland—and chefs like him—knew he could make Detroit Style without ever working the line at Buddy's; all he needed was an example and his own imagination. This is true of many Third Wave chefs: they learned through email conversations, blog posts, chat rooms, DMs and every other form of modern-day communication that the style was a viable platform for their creativity. When they needed information about an ingredient, a tweak to a recipe or a suggestion for a new set of toppings, someone would be there for them.

Gone were the days of sweating it out alone in a kitchen. The fear of your once-trusted dough guy walking off with the family recipe was over. Today's chefs carry a certain level of trust in one another but also in their own talents. They have culinary school, personal travel and the Internet. They don't hide their knowledge for fear that someone else will open up down the road and take all their customers or their ability to pay their bills. Rather, the Third Wave are vanguards, leading the way with new ideas and advancing Detroit Style with their own take on it, confident that what they do to the recipe will not only work but also taste better than their competition.

"I would DM people, and I still do," says Nate Peck, the chef who co-owns Michigan & Trumbull, a Detroit pizzeria that specializes in Detroit Style, with his partner, Kristen Calverley. "Some people would be generous and just lay it all out for me. And I do the same, too, when people ask me now, so I can return the favor."

Peck and Calverley, both Metro Detroit natives, started Michigan & Trumbull in Pittsburgh when they could not find the square pizza they loved in their new city. They started making their own version, modeled in part after the crunchy crust of Jet's, Buddy's and Emmy Squared.

Detroit itself also gained a kind of culinary confidence in this time frame. While the city always had its longtime restaurant icons, it gained a reputation among newly graduated chefs as a place where they could make a name for themselves faster or differently. That resulted in great pizzas—think of Dave Mancini's daily devotion to making every pie that his Supino Pizzeria served for years—as well as James Beard nominations and awards. Chefs who grew up in Metro Detroit and moved away came back; others stayed for the opportunity to own restaurants and build status, as entrepreneurs like Dan Gilbert rebuilt the city's office and residential real estate. While Detroit always had great pizza, it didn't always have that culinary-industry buzz. Now, it does. It even has pizza tours, led by cyclist Jason Hall, whose Herculin effort of eating pizza every day for a year came about because he's such a fan of Detroit pie.

Take Dave DeWall of Grandma Bob's in Detroit. With quiet confidence, the longtime chef says he wanted the most innovative Detroit Style pizza to come from within the city rather than a New York or San Francisco restaurant.

"My personal vision was: How can we pay tribute to this? But don't get me wrong; there's always going to be amazing Detroit Style pizzerias all over the country. But to me, it didn't really feel right that maybe the most innovative Detroit Style pizza places were not going to be in Detroit," DeWall says. "I felt like we owed it to the style and to the city to be among the people pushing the envelope of this style and keep that attention in Detroit.

"We're always playing around, trying to push the boundaries, specifically of what Detroit Style could be. Perfecting Detroit Style is really our goal, day in and day out, here," DeWall says. "We're constantly learning. The dough is a living, breathing thing, so there's always challenges.

"I talk to people all the time who haven't had Detroit Style pizza. Or if they have, it may not have been the best. No offense to some of the older places; I just think we're better in terms of the basics. We offer a more quality product in every aspect, and I think the guest notices that. So many people have not been exposed to this style yet—to what it can be," DeWall says.

Then there are chefs like Como's Zack Sklar. The chef grew up in Detroit but graduated from the Culinary Institute of America, "the Harvard of culinary schools," as he puts it. While he says he loves his hometown's pizza makers, including Jet's and Buddy's, he also sees the way he makes Detroit Style as a step above his competitors, whom he says are different than chefs like him.

"There are two cuisines that only of recent years have gone through a chef's lens, and that's barbecue and pizza," Sklar says. "With pizza, these recipes are very old, usually done by cooks, not chefs. I'm going to geek out about every topping, every nuance….With Buddy's and Jet's, you need scale. You don't have to be as trained to make those pizzas.

"This is my life's work, and I'm trained to think about this shit. I'm not taking anything away from them. I'm just building on top of it."

Sklar also says some of the Detroit Style pizza traditions—like the stories of the blue-steel automotive pans, how they're seasoned and how they're prepped—are antiquated.

"I've read stories where they say you have to buy seasoned blue-steel pans to make this. That's bullshit. It's such a joke," Sklar says. "They also say you shouldn't wash the pans. That's also gross. It's disgusting. Food doesn't taste better because you're cooking it in a dirty pan."

TWO KEY MOMENTS CHANGED the way we collectively view pizza. There was the shift after World War II when the United States fell in love with pizza and started eating it regularly. Eating out became a family outing that pleased not only mom, who didn't have to cook that night, but also everyone else's taste buds. Author and Chicago pizza tour operator Steve Dolinsky says this is when the different styles started to take hold. For example, the East Coast created a portable experience. "You grab and go and eat it while you're walking," Dolinsky says. The Midwest developed sit-down restaurants that were more like "appointment dining," Dolinsky says. "It evolved into a family mealtime." That seems true in Detroit and of its signature square pie. You can't eat it when you're walking because you truly need a table, chair, knife and fork for an optimal experience.

The second major change in pizza making came around in the late 1980s, when California chefs like Alice Waters and Wolfgang Puck started making artisan pizza. Then came Chris Bianco, who gained legendary status in the pizza world for perfecting every ingredient and technique in pizza. But his work led to a larger trend of trained chefs starting to make pizza. They all had certain things in common, like an obsessive care about the dough as well as the toppings. They had a renewed attention to detail when it came to the process. They focused largely on the crust, making it as perfect as possible to enable the toppings to shine. This renaissance gave rise to a foodie movement, which put a new lens on pizza. It was about interpreting pizza through local food culture, boosting attention to the maker as well as the final product.

For bread expert, cookbook author and pizza connoisseur Peter Reinhart, the focus on artisan pizza brought about a refinement of the process that took pizza out of the bakery and into the larger restaurant world.

"It starts with the crust. You can't have a great pizza if you don't have a great crust. No matter how good the toppings are, the pizza can only be interesting if the crust isn't great," Reinhart says. "But if you have a great

Pizza expert Steve Dolinsky has touted Detroit Style pizza as a real style, helping spread the word about it through his books and his podcast, *Pizza City*. *Steve Dolinsky*.

crust, it hardly matters what you put on top. A little sauce, a little cheese, people are going to come back for it, and it will become memorable, which began my definition of greatness."

Trade shows like the International Pizza Expo also changed pizza makers into pizzaiolos, elevated the status of the pizzeria. *PMQ* writer and test chef Brian Hernandez notes how the relationships that were built during these trade shows helped everyone up their pizza game. This free flow of ideas allowed people to learn faster and gain new skills they could bring home.

"You were getting ideas from people that weren't your competitors and were in other markets," Hernandez says. "That helped the industry grow because if you help the industry, it will help everybody."

Peter Lachapelle launched the International Pizza Expo in 1985, and the four-day event is now considered the largest pizza industry event in the world. There are classes, lectures and supplier booths as far as the eye can see, as well as networking events where lifelong friendships are made. It also is the home of the International Pizza Challenge and the World Pizza Games, where people like Tony Gemignani and Shawn Randazzo become industry celebrities. After all, many credit Randazzo's win in the Best of the

Peter Reinhart (*left*) and Shawn Randazzo spoke frequently for Reinhart's podcast and YouTube show, *Pizza Quest*. *Randazzo family.*

Best competition there as the reason Detroit Style escaped out of Detroit and into the wider world.

"Bottom line, you've never been to anything like Pizza Expo. It's a family reunion, a festival and B2B trade show," Lachapelle says. "It's a wild event."

Laura Meyer, a top pizza maker who works with Gemignani at his International Pizza School, agrees.

"Pizza competitions and the Pizza Expo have the people who really dictate trends as well as the direction of the pizza industry as a whole," Meyer says. "Certain figures earn trust within the pizza industry, and they're all ones that have roles at the pizza expos, who write books, who teach classes, who write articles for the pizza magazines. There's a lot of people who implicitly trust them based on that pedigree, including Tony, Smokevitch and Shawn Randazzo. They trust them and trust the product. They say, "Maybe I'll try that,' because they trust the source it comes from."

Detroit's longtime chains may have skipped the expos for a variety of reasons, Hernandez says. "They didn't come out of their bubble. They were probably happy with what they were doing, and they just wanted to maintain it. Because of that, they didn't grow....[That may be] why the name or style wasn't recognized quicker across the nation. What they were doing was good enough."

Lachapelle says not every pizzeria owner or every pizzaiolo, whether they are from Detroit or elsewhere, is going to attend an expo. But, he humbly believes, they all should.

"By default, most pizza makers don't compete. We only have room for about 225 to 250 competitors," he says. "Some want to push themselves to learn. Some don't want to see what they don't know. Pizza Expo is not the largest, but it is generally accepted as being the most important or prestigious....A competitor with a fragile ego may be intimidated."

THE THIRD WAVE KNOWS this. They go to the events. They attend the pizza schools. They follow one another on social media, studying photographs slavishly. But they don't want to be compared to Buddy's, Cloverleaf or Loui's. They reject the idea of copying "the original" or having to do exactly what the OGs did to create Detroit Style.

"They all liked the idea of it being different," says Scott Weiner, founder of New York–based Scott's Pizza Tours and noted pizza historian. "They're not looking to copy something or [make] something that sticks to the original recipe....There's a negativity to the use of the word 'authentic' or the dogma of the original recipe. These are chefs that want to be innovative. They take the things they like about something and tweak it to become something they like."

Brian Hernandez agrees: "I don't think Detroit Style pizza is a trend. It has been around since the 1940s. I look at it more as a well-kept secret. No one knows why it took so long to get recognition outside Michigan and the Midwest. But now that the secret is out, and [with] true pizzaiolo ego and drive for innovation, they look at it and say, 'I can do that, and better!'"

Outside of Michigan, Glenn Cybulski—and chefs like him—says his goal isn't to perfectly copy what the original Detroit Style restaurants do. Rather, he wants to give the people he cooks for his interpretation—and it will be delicious. For example, he prefers to "parbake" his Detroit Style crust, meaning he cooks it until it's about halfway done before adding the toppings—a practice some Detroit Style purists revile. The purists say you have to cook the dough raw and add the cheese, then the toppings and, finally, the sauce.

"We don't have to be as authentic as they do in Detroit. What I want to do is, I want to make sure people are tasting a phenomenal product that's called a Detroit Style pizza for all of those people who will never go to Detroit to taste it," Cybulski says. "They will have the closest experience they would if they went into a Buddy's or Cloverleaf and having a fresh pan pizza....I will replicate the product, and I will praise Detroit because of its entire process and the flavor profile that's so unbelievable. But I won't try to replicate that."

Even the creators of pizza's magnum opus only visited a few local pizzerias when they came to Detroit. The authors of *Modernist Pizza* went to more than 250 pizzerias all around the world, from Italy to the United States to Tokyo to Argentina. *Modernist Cuisine* creator Nathan Myhvold and chef Francisco Migoya created a three-volume book that covers the complete history of pizza and includes more than one thousand recipes. While they wanted to try the best in the Motor City while they were here, visiting Shawn Randazzo, they also went to places like Tony Gemignani's to try his Detroit Style pies, Migoya says.

"How can you say pizza that's not made in Detroit isn't traditional? What does that even mean?" Migoya says. "There's a resistance to anything in the world of pizza that isn't the style you grew up with. People feel strongly about where to get the best pizza, like a sports team. You support your team no matter what, whether they're good or bad. They're your team."

Myhvold spoke to this tribalism or extreme loyalty to your local sports team and pizza parlor as part of the *Modernist Pizza* PR tour: "We found that what makes great pizza to eat today isn't whether the place was famous one hundred years ago. In fact, in general, old, famous pizzerias are lousy. What you really need to have a great pizzeria is some energetic person who comes in to work every day and want to make the best pizza they possibly can."

That's why Myhvold considers Portland the best pizza city in the world. Not New York. Not Chicago. And certainly not Detroit. Portland doesn't have the emotional baggage or historical hang-ups these other cities do, he says.

To Hernandez, "Detroit still gets credit for originating and sustaining the popularity of this style," but he also recognizes the innovation happening outside of the city.

"I give credit to every other pizzeria outside of Michigan trying out their own Detroit recipes. It is definitely a team effort....You have to respect what the core of the pizza is and from there, make it your own. You have to put your own spin on it."

Chapter 13

BIG BUSINESS

*D*etroit Style Pizza has transformed from a local favorite into an internationally beloved menu item, showing up at pizzerias everywhere from Alaska to Dubai to Seoul. What started in Gus Guerra's small kitchen at Six and Conant in Detroit is now served by classically trained chefs, at pop-ups in buses and campers and in sit-down restaurants. Chefs have thrown themselves into the product, tweaking every aspect and topping the classic crust with morels, truffles and even gold leaf. It seems there is no end to the possibilities when it comes to this inherently Detroit style of pizza.

That begs the question: Is Detroit Style unique enough to be listed among the pantheon of pizza styles, like New York, Chicago, New Haven and Neapolitan? The answer is yes from all sources, whether it is pizzaiolos, pizza historians or just the average person on the street. Detroit Style has specific characteristics, distinct flavors, specialized ingredients and a legacy that befits a long-lasting style. Cookbooks are written about it. Recipes abound. Hashtags like #DetroitStylePizza are used hundreds of thousands of times on social media. Even the television reality show *Chopped* used Detroit Style pizza as an ingredient on one of its episodes.

Pizza chains have also taken on this product as their sole menu item or the highlight of their menu. As it stands, there are a number of chains that specialize in Detroit Style pizza, including Buddy's, Via 313, Emmy Squared and Blue Pan Pizza, which has multiple locations in Colorado. Buddy's

Blue Pan Pizza is Jeff Smokevitch and Giles Flanagin's restaurant tribute to Detroit Style pizza, and they now have multiple locations. *Blue Pan.*

and Via 313 now have venture capital backers and, in the case of Buddy's, corporate owners, all of whom are willing to pour hundreds of thousands of dollars into construction of new restaurants, training and marketing to see who can make Detroit Style a national brand first. At the same time, Jet's Pizza now has a massive franchise network with more than four hundred locations and the goal of hitting one thousand stores in the future.

This growth comes at a key time in the pizza industry. During the COVID-19 pandemic, pizza saw extreme success as people opted for takeout food, and pizza was the perfect solution. Chains like Domino's and Little Caesars drove growth across the industry, adding new technology to their delivery and takeout options even faster.

There's also been national competition along the way—in 2019, Pizza Hut introduced its first attempt at Detroit Style pizza. Having that sizable a company, and one with deep historic roots, take on Detroit's favorite square pizza as its latest menu item was both a blessing and a curse for Detroiters. It was an honor because it put Detroit Style on the national level, sparking new interest in the style and boosting its reputation. It was a negative, however, because the Pizza Hut version was different enough from what is produced in Detroit kitchens that it drew local and regional criticism for not meeting the standards set in the Motor City. Even Little Caesars decided to capitalize on Detroit Style's popularity, setting up a competition between itself and Pizza Hut in recent years.

Someone, sometime, will get it right. And when they do, there will be a Detroit Style chain that goes national. The only question is who will get there first.

IN 2018, A KANSAS-BASED private equity firm called CapitalSpring bought Buddy's from the Jacobs family. Robert Jacobs described the partnership as "a significant opportunity for us to introduce Buddy's iconic pizza, rich culture and community roots to new customers in Detroit and beyond." Buddy's had twelve restaurants and carryout locations at the time, and CapitalSpring promised to grow the brand well beyond the Midwest. CapitalSpring brought in a new CEO, a new CFO, a human resources director, a culinary director and a new vice president of operations to supervise the restaurants, which it described in media coverage as inconsistent and without a chain-wide identity.

CapitalSpring is a private investment firm that focuses on the restaurant industry. It is headquartered in Nashville and has offices in Los Angeles, Atlanta and New York. The firm has invested $2 billion in more than sixty brands across North America. In 2019, former Baja Fresh and Nando's executive Burton Heiss became Buddy's CEO, one of the first "outsiders" to run the brand.

"We're committed to focusing on what makes Buddy's special and leaning into that," Heiss said in a statement. "We're all about original Detroit-style pizza and how we can expose more people to what we feel is a spectacular brand....I don't see any limits to what we can do and where we can take Buddy's. Again, because of our exceptional core product that's unique and our verifiable provenance around Detroit-style pizza. It's about how we can grow organically and with purpose."

CapitalSpring also sold the original Buddy's location at Six and Conant, part of the way it wanted to fund the chain's expansion. In June 2019, a New Jersey–based firm, Essential Properties Realty Trust, bought the building for $1.36 million. Buddy's continues to operate out of the original location under a sale-leaseback agreement.

There have also been some growing pains. In September 2022, Buddy's announced it was closing its first Lansing location in Delta Township. The 6,350-square-foot pizzeria opened in June 2020. The company said through its local public relations firm, Franco, that the chain had "decided to consolidate operations to our Okemos full-service location."

For Via 313, those first years in Austin were a blur, the Hunt brothers say. Zane remembers how his IT job allowed him to work from home, and he regularly made dough between calls and meetings. He'd take a break and run the dough to the trailer, where Brandon was prepping for the evening shift. They opened a second trailer in 2013, starting at South Congress and then moving six months later to Rainey Street.

Both trailers were making money, but that goal of a sit-down restaurant continued to nag at them. By now, Brandon was working full time at Via 313, earning about $250 a week for his efforts. Zane wasn't taking a paycheck so they could put any remaining profits in the bank. They started looking at properties, and a place in Oak Hill came available. The only question was whether the Via 313 brand could translate from Austin's view of it as bar food or a "downtown thing" into a place families would visit, Zane says.

The timing started to make Zane question whether he could continue in his double life, doing his IT job during the day and helping Brandon at night. Zane went to his boss and spoke plainly: The brothers had two trailers and a restaurant coming. "This needed to work because this is what we're working for," Zane says. "Failure was not an option."

Zane's boss gave him the out he needed. The company had job cuts coming, and while Zane wasn't scheduled to be let go, his boss could put him on the list. Zane took the buyout and got enough funding through the redemption of his paid time off to be able to work full time at Via 313's Oak Hill location. Together, Zane and Brandon became co-general managers, and Zane could finally start taking a paycheck.

As opening day in 2015 approached, the two started to get nervous again. What if this was a mistake? What if this massive investment sat empty? What if Detroit Style pizza was a fluke? The pressure built, Zane says.

Turns out, they didn't need to worry.

"We had a line down the street the first day we opened the Oak Hill restaurant," Zane says.

Via 313 opened its North Campus restaurant in 2016; two years later, its East Sixth Street location launched. In the years that followed, Via 313 was dubbed "one of the very best pizzas" by *Food and Wine Magazine*, named Independent Pizzeria of the Year by *Pizza Today* magazine and recognized as one of the Top 10 Pizzas in America by Food Network.

The brand grew enough that the Hunt brothers started to think about finding a partner that could help them with finding new locations and give them the support they needed to make their Detroit Style pizza restaurant the national chain they wanted it to be.

In 2020, Zane and Brandon announced they were partnering with the Savory Fund. That year, Savory invested $100 million in several restaurants and businesses, including Via 313. The partnership gave the Hunt brothers access to a team of restaurant-industry veterans, who had the experience to develop the chain into a larger entity. It was a huge year for the brothers, who also gained national fame when *Pizza Today* magazine named the company Independent Pizzeria of the Year.

That Savory investment would allow Via 313 to go national. The goal was to more than double in size. The pizza company grew outside of Texas for the first time, adding three locations in Utah, where Savory is based.

"It is one of the most exciting times in the pizza industry. Over the past decade, there has been a lot of disruption with fast-casual pizza concepts and low-cost pizza options. None have been more interesting, nostalgic and quality-driven [than] Via 313," said Andrew K. Smith, managing director of the Savory Fund, in a press release. "Detroit Style Pizza is one of the best-kept secrets, and we can't wait to bring it to more communities in Texas, Utah, and additional states that will be announced soon!"

In 2022, Via 313 and the Savory Fund hired Ray Risley, a veteran restaurant leader, as the brand's chief executive officer overseeing its twelve locations. Along with serving as the original Spago's general manager working alongside Wolfgang Puck, Risley had helped expand multiple restaurants and boost their revenues by double and triple digits. "Ultimately, Ray was the right person to guide Via 313 into our explosive growth plan," the Hunt brothers said in a statement.

Jet's Pizza continued its nationwide expansion in 2022 with its four hundredth location; the Chicago site in the Jefferson Park neighborhood opened that July. John Jett, Jeff Galloway and Jim Galloway all attended the grand opening to help celebrate the milestone.

During this monumental event, Jet's announced its plans to add thirty more locations, introducing the brand to Utah, Kansas, New Mexico, Washington and Nevada. There are Jet's Pizza franchises in nineteen states to date.

"It's incredible to think we just opened our 400th location when it feels like just yesterday I was sitting on milk crates with my brother, Eugene, outside our first location, dreaming of this," John Jetts told reporters.

What made the moment bittersweet was knowing Eugene wasn't there to celebrate with them; Eugene died of cancer in 2014. He was sixty years old.

"I really wish my brother was here today to see what's going on. That's the tough part," John says.

ALL THE HISTORIC DETROIT Style restaurants made efforts to expand, only to find that spreading themselves too thin caused family rifts and challenges they did not anticipate. Cloverleaf opened multiple franchises, but Jack Guerra sold them in 2020.

At one point, Loui's tried to expand to another location, opening a carryout restaurant at Wattles and John R. in Troy. Managing two pizza joints amid family illness turned out to be too challenging, Nykolas said. "My grandpa was ripping his hair out" trying to manage both spots. The family decided to let that location go and focus solely on Hazel Park as its home.

In an interview, Louis noted the challenges of expansion: "It wouldn't work. You can bottle the sauce. You can ship barrels of dough. But how do you package these?" he told *Detroit News* reporter Jim Treloar, holding up his own two hands.

The one thing Nykolas knows is that he will never change the pizza or its style.

"I think of it as a theme restaurant. This is a 1970s themed restaurant. You come in here and it's a blast from the past," Nykolas says. "This is how it's supposed to be....It helps me remember my grandpa. He was my best friend."

Shield's also opened and closed a few locations—but with another family at the helm. Brothers Paul and Peter Andoni purchased the chain from their cousins, the Moraitises, in 1992. Paul calls Detroit Style pizza the backbone of their restaurants.

"It's in my blood. It's a challenging business, but it's in my blood," Paul says.

OTHER PEOPLE HAVE SPARKED huge interest in Detroit Style pizza simply by eating a slice and sharing their opinion on social media. One of them is Dave Portnoy, who started the popular *Barstool Sports* blog and publicizes pizza places through his "one-bite reviews" on YouTube. After a high rating from Portnoy, Detroit Style Pizza chains like Randazzo's Detroit Style Pizza Company saw their sales go through the roof. In April 2020, Portnoy tried one of the pies at Detroit Style Pizza Company and gave Shawn's pizza an 8.7, which is one of the highest scores he had granted at that point. After that review was posted online, Linda Michaels remembers the carryout was slammed for weeks and it took months to catch up on frozen orders.

Shawn Randazzo was diagnosed with brain cancer in 2020 and passed away in December of that year. He left behind his wife, Keri, and children Angelina, Harmony, Dominic and Trinity and granddaughter Mariah. *Randazzo family.*

That national recognition was among the highlights of Shawn's career. But it also came at one of the lowest points of his life. Shawn was diagnosed with stage four glioblastoma in late 2019. He started treatment shortly thereafter, having surgery in December 2019 to remove a brain tumor and needing radiation and chemotherapy. In an article for the *Detroit News* about the *Barstool* review, Shawn said: "It's been challenging. But I'm grateful to be alive and I've got a lot to fight for. I've got a beautiful family and a business that is just growing right and I'm not going anywhere soon."

The illness progressed aggressively, and Shawn died on December 5, 2020. He was forty-four years old.

His death led to an outpouring of respect within the pizza industry. Pizzerias named pies after him. The Pizza Expo created a Shawn Randazzo award. Tributes poured into Keri Randazzo's email, social media and telephone—along with some offers to buy the business out from under her. Thankfully, Shawn's mom, Linda, and Keri still own the business and are now franchising it on their own.

Shawn's life wasn't an overnight success. But, in death, his contributions to Detroit Style pizza were cemented.

"I think Shawn is singlehandedly responsible for the resurgence of this style's popularity in the past ten years," says *PMQ*'s Brian Hernandez. "He provided a lot of knowledge and access to tools and pans that people weren't regularly producing or selling at the time."

The Randazzo family have started a franchise, Corktown Pizza, which has pictures of Shawn hanging in the restaurant. Keri Randazzo is one of the co-owners of this new family enterprise. *Randazzo family.*

Glenn Cybulski agrees. "Shawn is responsible for the popularity and the expansion of Detroit Style pizza today, period. Any of the OGs can say what they want. Shawn made it happen."

In fact, Shawn's life had a huge impact on the pizza industry, according to Laura Meyer.

"Shawn's win showed the capacity and the effect of the Pizza Expo as well as the effect of what one person could do and the resounding ripple effect you can have," Meyer says. "This was his product. He believed in it. He believed in the possibilities. He was willing to share that with anybody—if you wanted to know about it, he was so excited because someone else wanted to participate….He bent over backward for you with no catch. His legacy will go on."

Most people wouldn't know what Detroit Style was without Shawn, Peter Lachapelle believes.

"Shawn put it on the map. He had the greatest impact on the industry in the past decade," Lachapelle says. "He did not wear the badge that he was a great pizzaiolo. He did have the greatest impact on the pizza industry in the past decade."

Tony Gemignani says he believed in Shawn's talent so much that he put the young pizza maker in his book *The Pizza Bible*.

"The people in Detroit should really celebrate him. He believed in the pizza. He wanted to make it better. He strived to make it better," Gemignani says. "Where could he have been? How far could he have gone? He went to the end, positive he'd be here tomorrow."

Shawn's family continues to honor his memory and grow his legacy. That desire to see his recognition continue got a new foundation in 2022 when they opened their first franchise, Corktown Pizza in Petoskey, finally turning Shawn's dream of a large pizza company based on Detroit Style into reality.

Chapter 14

ORIGINAL VERSUS AUTHENTIC

*I*t could be said that Detroit Style pizza took more than six decades to go from an idea to a verified pizza style. What happened next was unsurprising, in some ways—when it finally gained a national and then international fan base, fans, amateur cooks and professional chefs started to change the recipe. That led to a debate: Who is the original? Who can say they make authentic Detroit Style pizza? And, more importantly, what is the difference between an imitator and an innovator?

Those questions are significant—so much so that at one point, Buddy's Pizza threatened to sue Cloverleaf for using the term "original." This forced Cloverleaf's attorney to determine through state records and alcohol licenses that Gus Guerra indeed owned Buddy's and created its first pizzas, allowing Cloverleaf to use that term in its marketing and advertising. So, if you were wondering if these two businesses are passionate about what they do and who else should be "allowed" to do it, that should answer your question.

Now, we get into the weeds. For most pizza aficionados, "original" means the first or one of the earliest versions. In this case, Buddy's Rendezvous, in 1946, made the original Detroit Style pizza. Gus Guerra, who made that first pizza, was its original creator, and he brought his recipe to Cloverleaf. End of story.

"We are the original Detroit Style pizza as it was originally formulated and made," says Wes Pikula of Buddy's Pizza. "There were people who left Buddy's and put their own spin on it because they thought it would be better or because they didn't know the recipe completely. But there's really nobody out there that's still doing it from scratch like the way we started doing it....

In fact, ownership was rabid about not touching or changing it. In fact, they were afraid of changing it."

"Authentic" means a reliable or genuine version of the original. For argument's sake, it can be said that Louis Tourtois made authentic Detroit Style when he started making pizza at Shield's. Louis always kept some of the secrets to his version of Buddy's pizza to himself, and that remained true when he started doing the food side at Shield's.

Some people, including Ian G. Duncan, note that many in the pizza community agree that Buddy's and its direct descendants—Loui's and Shawn Randazzo's Detroit Style Pizza Company in particular—also can be considered authentic. Ian adds Shawn to this venerable list because he learned the style from the Guerra family, tweaking the dough recipe to make it his own.

Others, such as Joseph Maino, who worked at Detroit Style Pizza Company with Shawn, agree.

"Thanks to Shawn Randazzo, we were given some criteria that helped lead us in the 'authentic' direction," Maino says. "Authentic meaning well-hydrated Sicilian-style dough pressed out and risen twice in a seasoned steel pan, lightly oiled. Caramelized Wisconsin brick cheese edge to edge. Pepperoni underneath the cheese. Sauce on top. All baked from a fresh dough, leading to a crown of caramelized cheese, not a wall of cheese that easily separates from the crust when using a parbaked dough."

Gus Guerra hand sliced his pepperoni for years, finally going to a machine when he could. He always made his Detroit Style with heart and passion for it, his family says. *Guerra family.*

The main question seems to be: Can you change the recipes of the original or authentic styles and still call your pie a Detroit Style pizza? A question that's equally important to those who make this style of pizza in Detroit: How does Detroit make sure it doesn't get forgotten in this new world of pizza cities and styles?

"'Authentic' should be used by other shops in Detroit that picked up the idea and created their own unique version of an authentic Detroit Style pizza," Duncan says. "Detroit Style pizza has almost become the pizza equivalent of Xerox or Kleenex."

Multiple companies, including Via 313 and Detroit Style Pizza Co., have thought about or tried to trademark the "Detroit Style pizza" term—and most legal entities reject this, noting that it cannot be trademarked because it is a descriptive term.

Additionally, there's no larger entity that can settle the debate, either. Detroit never created an official board of review or standards like the True Neapolitan Pizza Association (Associazione Verace Pizza Napoletana or AVPN) has for Neapolitan-style pizza. Since June 1984, Neapolitan pizza makers have worked under this nonprofit organization, whose mission is "to promote and protect in Italy and worldwide the true Neapolitan pizza." So, without an organized body willing to take on the challenge of setting a "DSP" standard, there is no way to authenticate what is a Detroit Style pizza other than what people in the First Wave or, arguably, those aligned with the Second Wave agree on generally.

For Skip McClatchy, the shape is one of the key components. "The dough recipe is really very basic, and I know many cooks take the basic recipe and add to it and it is still authentic," the former co-owner of Sabina's says. "I would say as long as they are baked in a square pan and use a full-body cheese (when the oil drips down the pan to make that crisp edge) I would consider it being true to the original Detroit Style square pizza."

However, Maino says he believes there is room for innovators as long as the common theme of Detroit's traditional approach has its day.

"I no longer believe you have to follow these exact processes in order to call it a Detroit 'Style' pizza," Maino says. "As long as you are baking a pizza in a rectangular pan with caramelized cheese around the edge and sauce on top, then you're making a Detroit Style pizza. On occasion, I even make parbaked shells at home to achieve a more advanced texture or have the convenience of pulling a shell from the freezer whenever I choose to have pizza."

There is an exception to this, Maino admits: "I want anyone who wins the Shawn Randazzo award at the International Pizza Expo in Las Vegas to have done it with a fresh dough, not a parbake."

EPILOGUE

What will happen next for Detroit and its pizza? Hard to say, and it would likely be foolhardy to write down any predictions—the food world is fickle, and tastes can change in an instant. Still, with so many fans worldwide, one thing is clear: people will continue to eat this delicious creation, no matter where it is made.

After all, it took more than half a century to get here, and Detroit has proven it has staying power—and, it should be noted, a long memory, so don't try to take Detroit out of the pizza it created, maintained and now shares with the world.

"With certain styles that really take hold, it takes time. It doesn't blow up overnight. You can see how [Detroit Style pizza] has taken time to take root and now is accessible in most major cities. It's something people want. They ask for it now," says Laura Meyer, Tony Gemignani's longtime pizza maker and now pizzeria owner.

"It's not just major city people who are asking for it. Now, the chains are getting in on it. Now, it's in the frozen food section of your grocery store. That means there's a demand for it," Meyer says. "It's amazing that Detroit Style pizza is there. That's how you know that you've got something—when someone wants to duplicate your item and mass produce it. That's how you know you've really made it."

Detroit made something great—and its pizza deserves recognition, agrees Brian Hernandez of *PMQ* magazine.

"Detroit is a very determined city," Hernandez says. "They have to innovate to stand out and keep up with the rest of the world, as do other cities, but innovation in pizza is something that is very contagious."

At its heart, says Emmy Squared's Howard Greenstone, the story of Detroit Style pizza always has to go back to that of Gus Guerra, who created a pizza that is now legendary.

"A country's culture and history are found in its food. When it comes to Detroit Style pizza, it's part of Americana. This was Gus's American dream," Greenstone says.

Wes Pikula says it best, so he gets the final word.

"This pizza belongs to Detroit just like the car belongs to Detroit. Just like Motown music belongs to Detroit," Pikula says. "When you've got love for this sort of pizza—that's what makes it....It's getting up, every day, and doing the work. And that's something that should never be forgotten."

Appendix

MIKE SPURLOCK'S DETROIT STYLE PIZZA RECIPE

Mike Spurlock's Pizza Sauce

1 (28-oz) can San Marzano tomatoes
½ tablespoon dried basil leaf
½ tablespoon dried oregano
½ teaspoon granulated garlic powder
1 teaspoon salt

This recipe makes a relatively small batch of sauce, but it should provide plenty of flavorful marinara to cover three or four eight-square pizzas, depending on how "saucy" you like your pizza.

Making good sauce is as simple as adding the ingredients to a stainless steel or ceramic-coated pot and using an immersion blender to shred and combine the tomatoes and other spices thoroughly. If you don't have an immersion blender, you can use a regular blender or food processor. You can use a low grind or pulse setting to avoid unnecessarily bruising the tomatoes and creating a bunch of foam or froth. If you like your sauce a little chunkier, skip the blender. The tomatoes will break down, but the sauce won't be as thin.

From there, set the pot on low heat and stir using a wooden or other nonreactive spoon. Stir about every 15–20 minutes for approximately 2–4 hours. The objective here is not to completely boil down the sauce but rather to cook some of the water out of it so when it's applied to the pizza, you don't end up with water running everywhere. The other main objective here is to concentrate the flavors. As the sauce thickens and you get rid of the excess water, the flavors from the spices and tomatoes will really stand out. You'll know when the sauce is ready because it will become substantially thicker, rich and flavorful.

The "Loui Loui" Detroit Style Pizza

This recipe will produce two eight-square pizzas, so remember to cut the quantities below in half for the amounts to be used for each pizza.

32 oz. Detroit Style pizza dough
24 pieces deli-style pepperoni, sliced large
24 pieces Canadian bacon, sliced deli style
32 oz. Detroit Style pizza shredded cheese mix
16 oz. mild Italian sausage, crumbled
12 oz. fresh portobello mushrooms, sliced
1 (10–12 oz.) fresh white onion, diced large
6 oz. ripe black olives, pitted and sliced
1 (8–10 oz.) fresh green pepper, sliced large
16 oz. Mike Spurlock's Pizza Sauce

Assembly, Baking and Finishing Procedures

Preheat your oven to between 500 and 550 degrees Fahrenheit (use 550 degrees if your oven will go that high). While a pizza stone is not required, if you have one, place it in the oven and place the pan on the stone when you are ready to bake the pizza. Preheating the stone in the oven can help the bottom of the crust bake quickly and more evenly.

Coat the inside of the pan with nonstick vegetable spray, pan release or extra virgin olive oil. Spread the dough in the pan, taking care not to touch the dough too much. Cover the pan with a lid or kitchen wrap and allow the dough to proof until it reaches the edges of the pan, 4 to 6 hours. When fully proofed, the dough should be bubbly and reach the edges of the pan.

Carefully place the pepperoni slices onto the dough, taking care not to push the air out of the dough. Overlap the pepperoni if necessary, but try to ensure every bite will contain pepperoni. Repeat this procedure for the Canadian bacon.

Sprinkle the cheese over the meats and dough. Push some cheese into the corners and edges of the pan to ensure the entire pizza is covered with cheese. Use a little more against the edges of the pan to ensure thick, crunchy edges.

Sprinkle the crumbled Italian sausage over the cheese to ensure even coverage. Do the same for the mushrooms, diced onion, green pepper and black olives.

Place the pizza in the oven and bake for approximately six minutes. Turn the pizza carefully using oven mittens to help ensure the pizza bakes evenly, front to back. Bake for another six minutes, then check the pizza. Slowly open the oven door and stand back to let the steam dissipate—don't stick your face in front of the oven to look at the pizza until the steam has been released. Carefully remove the pizza from the oven and check the edges and center for doneness, as follows. Take a firm spatula and separate the edges of the crust from the pan. Carefully lift up the pizza to check the bottom. The bottom should be golden brown in appearance, and the edges should be firm. Place the pizza back in the oven for 3- to 5-minute increments as necessary to ensure the edges, bottom and cheese appear to be done. Remember that this pizza uses a good number of vegetables that produce steam when baked—take care opening the oven so you do not get burned by the steam.

When the pizza is fully baked, remove it from the oven and let it rest for 2 to 3 minutes. Using a kitchen mitten and firm spatula, again separate the pizza from the edges and bottom of the pan and transfer the entire pizza to a cutting board or pizza peel.

Cut each pizza into eight even slices. Ladle a dollop of sauce onto each slice. Some guests may prefer no sauce, and it's always good to ask before you apply the sauce. However, this pizza is simply awesome with lots of sauce on top of each slice.

ABOUT THE AUTHOR

*K*aren Dybis is a reporter who has covered Detroit through a number of publications, including the *Detroit News*. She also has been a freelance writer for many more, including *Time* magazine, *U.S. News & World Report* and jewelry-industry giant *JCK*. Her books include a history of the city's potato chip companies (*Better Made in Michigan*), an in-depth look at a 1931 murder mystery (*The Witch of Delray*) and a study of drive-in movie palaces (*The Ford-Wyoming Drive-In*). She also wrote a travel guide to the city called *Secret Detroit*.